PERFECT
PASTA

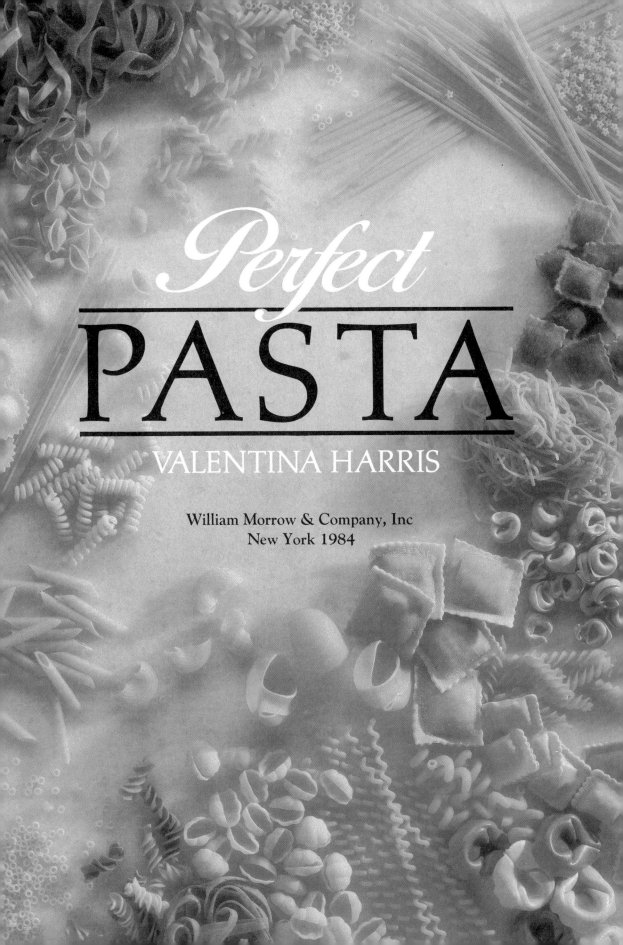

Perfect
PASTA

VALENTINA HARRIS

William Morrow & Company, Inc
New York 1984

This book was written at a difficult time and without the fantastic support
and help of all those around me it could never have been accomplished.
In particular, I want to dedicate this book to my husband, Bob,
with all the love in the world.
And special thanks to Jill Kennington for her brilliant idea,
without which this book would never have happened.

NOTES

Recipes serve 4 people unless
otherwise stated. 3½oz of pasta
is allowed per person. This is
suitable for a main course
serving. If the dish is to be served
as a starter allow 2oz per person.

Cooking times for pasta are
covered in The Golden Rules for
Cooking Pasta, page 15.

Freshly ground black pepper and
fresh herbs should be used
whenever possible.

Produced and designed by Shuckburgh Reynolds Ltd
Copyright © Text: Valentina Harris 1984
Copyright © Design: Shuckburgh Reynolds Ltd 1984

Library of Congress Catalog Card Number: 84-60324
ISBN 0-688-03929-4

Printed in Spain
by Printer industria gráfica s.a.
D.L.B. 21083-1984
First U.S. Edition
1 2 3 4 5 6 7 8 9 10

CONTENTS

THE PASTA COOK'S KITCHEN

There are certain basic ingredients and utensils which an Italian kitchen would never be without and which you should try to have on hand if you are planning to cook a lot of pasta. One of pasta's many qualities is that it acts as the catalyst which will turn a motley collection of ingredients into a dish fit for a king. Many of these ingredients are available in canned or dried form so a well-stocked pantry will enable you to conjure up a masterpiece without even a visit to the shops! Of course, if you have a freezer, you can also make sauces and complete baked dishes in advance and freeze them and keep a constant supply of different types of fresh pasta.

The following list of tools and ingredients should help you to be prepared for any eventuality:

KITCHEN UTENSILS

A large saucepan for cooking your pasta in at all times (unless you are cooking really small amounts for one person). It must hold 3 quarts of water for every 1lb of pasta and the pasta must be able to move freely while it cooks.

A long-handled fork to stir the pasta around as it cooks.

A perforated spoon or rounded fish slice to scoop out and drain certain types of pasta without having to drain the whole pot, e.g. *lasagne*, *tortellini* etc.

A sensible colander, preferably one with legs that will stand up by itself in the sink. Made of metal, preferably aluminium, and big enough to take up to 2lbs of pasta at one time. It should also have handles.

A medium-sized, single-handed, heavy-bottomed saucepan in which to make your sauces.

A cheese grater, preferably one with a tray into which the cheese falls as you grate it.

A good sharp knife or *mezzaluna* for chopping onions, herbs, carrots etc.

A wooden chopping board.

A mouli vegetable mill, which is indispensable (unless you have a food processor) for puréeing sauces and tomatoes.

Lots of wooden spoons for mixing, stirring and tasting your sauces.

FOR MAKING FRESH PASTA

A large pastry board, table top or other steady surface. Plastic pasta boards are now available and work quite well, but do not use marble as the surface is not suitable.

A rolling pin, which should be made of wood, about 30in long and about 1½in wide. Always keep your rolling pin oiled and lightly floured when not in use and it will last you for ever. Keep it hanging up in your kitchen so that it can breathe rather than shut up in a drawer.

A pastry wheel, for cutting pasta with wavy edges.

Ravioli cutters, both the tray variety (Raviolilamp) and the circular cutters.

A good knife with a broad blade for cutting pasta evenly and steadily.

Clean, fresh dishcloths for keeping the pasta on or underneath.

THE PANTRY

Cans of tomatoes in various sizes.

Cartons of puréed tomatoes. These are more expensive than canned tomatoes, but they do save time. Once opened, keep in the refrigerator.

Tomato paste. If you buy a can, remove any leftover and store in another container in the refrigerator once opened. Or keep the tubed variety and still store in the refrigerator once opened. Although Northern cooks are dreadfully rude about the "terrone" from down South who use tomato paste in their pasta sauces, I consider it to be a useful and practical ingredient. It is particularly good in sauces which are rich and thick, Bolognese for example.

Fresh garlic.

Nutmeg.

Dried herbs including oregano, marjoram, parsley, rosemary and bay leaves. Basil is the only herb which cannot be dried satisfactorily and the varieties available are just not worth eating. It is better to buy or make a jar of *Pesto* Sauce to keep in the refrigerator and substitute a little of this if basil is called for in the winter months.

Dried chilies.

Cans of tuna fish, sardines, anchovies and salmon.

Jars of olives and capers.

1 tinned truffle (in case the boss comes to dinner).

Rock salt.

Black peppercorns, for freshly ground black pepper.

Dried mushrooms, (*funghi porcini*, ceps), which will keep for ages in a paper bag.

Olive oil. Italian or Greek olive oil are best for pasta as they are stronger. The subtle taste of French oil tends to get lost amongst the other strong flavors.

Dried durum wheat pasta. Keep a selection of packages of various sizes and shapes. A 1lb package will serve five people, so if you might have to cater for more remember to have at least two packages of each type.

The list of possible pantry items is endless. My advice is to build up gradually. Buy a few things at a time and see which get used. It is a pointless waste of time and money to fill it to the brim only to have to throw mouldy objects and rusty cans away. To my mind, the only really important things are the pasta itself, tomatoes, garlic and olive oil.

THE REFRIGERATOR

Parmesan cheese. At home in Italy we keep the Parmesan with its grater in the pantry. If you live in a wet climate this may not work as the cheese goes mouldy, so keep it tightly wrapped in the refrigerator.

Pecorino cheese, also tightly wrapped.

A jar of ready-made *Pesto* Sauce (see recipe p.48).

A jug of household stock (see recipe p.14).

A bottle of Tomato Sauce (see recipe p.13).

Carrots, celery and onions, the basis for many sauces.

Fresh herbs, parsley and basil at least, standing upright in a glass of cold water.

A jar of dripping, into which you tip all the excess fat from your roasts. Once settled, a delicious meat jelly forms at the bottom of the jar which can be used in countless pasta recipes.

Tomatoes. The only tomatoes worth using with pasta are the elongated, San Marzano or similar types. Do not try using the large Italian salad tomatoes for cooking pasta sauces. Firm, ripe round tomatoes can be used particularly if they are cheap or you have a glut in the garden, but the flavor is not as good as plum tomatoes. To use fresh tomatoes you should remove the peel and seeds as follows. Pour boiling water over the tomatoes in a bowl and leave for 10 seconds (longer if they are slightly unripe). Drain the water and refill with cold water. Take out the tomatoes and peel off the skin with your fingers. Cut in half and scoop out the seeds. Pass through a vegetable mill or process quickly to reduce to a fresh tomato purée.

THE FREEZER

Parmesan and *Pecorino*. Grate and freeze small amounts in plastic bags.

Pesto (see page 48). Make lots of it when fresh basil is around and then serve it in the snowy winter for a taste of summer.

Plain tomato sauce (see page 12). Superb on its own, it can also be used as a base for other sauces.

Various ready-made sauces. Get into the habit of doubling the quantities when you make a sauce and put half in the freezer. But do not add garlic to any sauce which is to be frozen as it sometimes develops a rancid flavor.

A selection of oven-ready baked pasta dishes.

Stuffed pasta. Freeze quantities of 14oz, which is enough to feed four people.

Freshly made egg pasta. Freeze as for stuffed pasta.

CHEESES

PARMESAN

The king of the cheeses that are eaten with and on pasta has to be Parmesan. This superb, golden, crumbly, hard-grating cheese has been made in Italy for nearly 1000 years. In Italy it is usually called *Parmigiano*, which means it comes from the Parma region, or *grana*, which is a cheaper type of cheese. Parmesan has to be matured for at least two years before it is sold to the shops. The older the cheese, the harder and stronger-tasting it will be. It is only made in certain parts of Italy, mainly Reggio Emilia, some parts of Bologna and Modena, and the very best is produced in Parma itself. It is made from April to November and once made the factories keep the huge cheeses in special safes – yes, Italy even has cheese thieves! *Grana Padano* is generally considered not to be as good as *Parmigiano*. You can see what you are using if you read the lettering stamped on the outside of the hard crust.

Parmesan is made from cow's milk and has a high protein content and a fat content of 30%. It is the cheese most widely used with pasta and is best when grated fresh as and when you need it, or kept grated in the freezer. You can also buy it ready grated but there is absolutely no comparison between that and the real thing. Parmesan is normally added, grated, to the pasta as it is dressed and also served separately with the pasta, but it is also good on its own at the end of the meal with bread or fruit.

PECORINO

In order of importance Parmesan is closely followed by *pecorino*. This very strong cheese is made from ewe's milk and the most widely used variety is *pecorino Romano*, which you can sometimes find studded with peppercorns to make it even more strong in flavor. It is used mostly to enhance and invigor spicy, robust dishes like *Bucatini all'Amatriciana*. Other types of *pecorino* are *pecorino Sardo*, which is almost always eaten fresh and soft at the end of a meal, and *pecorino Siciliano*, sometimes known as *Canestrato*, which can either be eaten grated or sliced fresh.

RICOTTA

This creamy, pure white substance, made from the discarded whey of other cheeses such as *mozzarella* and *provolone*, only just makes it into the cheese category. It is very widely used in the preparation of pasta dishes, both as a filling in stuffed pasta and as an ingredient in many sauces. It can also be used in many sweet dishes and cakes, as it is not salted and has a very mild flavor. You may also come across *ricotta* that has been dried and baked; this can then be grated and tastes very salty.

MOZZARELLA

The best *mozzarella* is made from the milk of the water buffalo and is called *mozzarella di bufala*, but can usually only be found in specialist shops, even in Italy. It is a pure white cheese which will only keep for a few days in a bowl filled half with milk and half with water. It has a mild, creamy and very distinctive flavor and is normally rounded or pear-shaped. Beware of a strange grey substance which is sold under the name of *mozzarella* in rectangular slabs shrink-wrapped in hard plastic. This rubbery invention does not feel or taste remotely like *mozzarella*.

GORGONZOLA

This is Italy's blue cheese and the best kind has a runny consistency like ripe Brie: when it is like this it is said to have '*la goccia*'. If you have not yet tried my *Spaghetti al Gorgonzola* (page 44) you are in for a special treat!

PROVOLONE

The biggest of all Italian cheese, it has a huge cylindrical shape and is wrapped with string in order to hang it up. There are two varieties of this cheese: one is mild and sweet, *provolone dolce*, while the other is very peppery and fairly strong, *provolone piccante*. Not many pasta recipes call for this cheese and, if they do, either kind will do.

MASCARPONE

This too is hardly a cheese at all, being more like clotted cream. It is mainly used for desserts, but some pasta recipes call for it. If you have trouble finding it you can substitute a mixture of rich heavy cream and cream cheese or a full fat cream cheese. Philadelphia is also a good substitute.

PRESERVED MEATS

SALAME
This is not salami, but *salame*. It is strictly Italian and there are hundreds of different types. It is always dark red with spots of white fat. Never buy *salame* which is tough or dry, or hard when you squeeze it. My advice is to buy one of those short stubby cylinders called *salamino* and keep it wrapped in the refrigerator. Slice it as you need it, but eat it within a month.

PROSCIUTTO CRUDO
This is often incorrectly referred to as Parma ham. The literal translation is 'raw ham' and that is precisely what it is, a haunch of pork that has been hung up to ripen and gradually turn into this delicious type of ham. There are many different kinds of *prosciutto crudo* apart from the Parma variety. All are ready to eat.

PROSCIUTTO COTTO
This is cooked ham, softly pink and highly flavored. Italian ham takes a lot of beating, so when using ham for these recipes, take the trouble to get the best kind you can afford.

MORTADELLA
A huge pink roll of preserved meat, also pork, which has quite big white spots of fat and sometimes has pieces of pistachio in it. In Germany they make something very similar which can be used as a substitute.

BACON
In Italy bacon as we know it does not exist, although it is now imported and can be bought in certain shops. Instead they use that part of the pig to make *pancetta* or *guanciale*, which you buy in solid pieces and cut as you need it. I have used ordinary bacon in all these recipes and it works just as well, but in some cases it should be cut more thickly.

SAUSAGES
Most of the recipes calling for sausages require the little, plump, coarse Italian sausages which can be bought in specialist Italian delicatessens. If you cannot get them, you can obtain a similar taste, but not the texture, from a strong peppery sausage.

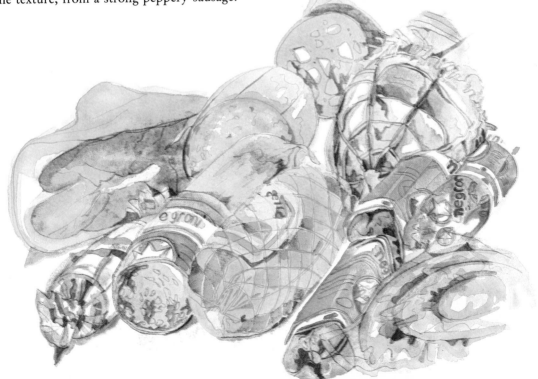

SERVING AND ACCOMPANIMENTS

Every day new recipes and ways of eating and serving pasta are invented. Without a doubt it is now generally accepted that with pasta, anything goes! I myself prefer to eat pasta in the traditional way. I find it very comforting when the steaming bowl of pasta is passed around the table in the old way of my childhood, when a sign of being grown up was to be allowed to help yourself for the first time. But mine is a highly personal opinion. There are many new recipes for pasta which contain unusual ingredients, are quick to prepare and taste delicious.

Basically, when it comes to cooking and serving pasta, you must do as your spirit takes you. There are just two standard rules I must insist upon: firstly, unless it is a cold dish pasta must be served as piping hot as possible, which all depends on speed in draining, dressing and serving it, and secondly, it must NOT be overcooked.

Traditionally, pasta is served as a starter to a meal. More often than not, *pasta asciutta* is served at lunchtime (so that you can recover from the largest meal of the day during your siesta!) and pasta soups are served in the evening. *Pasta asciutta*, which literally means 'dry pasta', that is pasta which is not in a soup, is the term used to describe dishes which are boiled and dressed with a sauce rather than baked or stuffed pasta.

If you are eating pasta as a first course, plan what is to follow with some care, as it is usually quite filling. A dish of ratatouille with salad and bread or some interesting omelettes are usually quite sufficient. In Italy, *Saltimbocca alla Romana* (fine veal cutlets with sage, prosciutto and mozzarella) or *Cotolette alla Milanese* (fine flattened veal, turkey breast or chicken breast tossed in breadcrumbs and lightly fried) are usual second courses. An unpretentious roast chicken or fish with lemon juice and herbs would also follow well. If you are serving meat as a second course be sure it does not have a heavy, rich sauce and if it does have a sauce make sure it is nothing like the sauce on the pasta. In many recipes for pasta with meat, the meat which was cooked and from which the sauce was created is often served either with the pasta or as a second course with a vegetable or salad.

Nowadays, pasta is often presented as a single-dish meal, accompanied by a salad and bread. Hot garlic bread or herb bread often go very well with it and if you serve pasta in this way for a supper party you can round off the meal with a light, tasty dessert. It is also a good idea when making pasta for large numbers to provide two or three different kinds, so there is something for everyone.

HOW TO SERVE PASTA

There are several ways of serving *pasta asciutta* and there is much debate in Italy over the correct form. The first, and most common way of presenting it, is to dress the pasta with the sauce in a bowl from which it is easy to extract the pasta. Pour a little sauce over the top, sprinkle on a little grated cheese and serve by passing the bowl around the table for people to help themselves. The second method is to dress the pasta in a bowl, transfer it to a flat platter, pour on a little sauce and sprinkle on some cheese. It is thought that in this way people can serve themselves more easily and that the flat dish shows off the pasta better. A third way is to dress the pasta in a serving bowl or dish with a minimum of sauce and to send the rest of the sauce to the table in a sauce boat or bowl. In this way, people can add as much sauce as they like to their portion.

Some households, however, favor the method adopted by many Italian restaurants, where the plain boiled pasta is arranged on individual plates and a ladleful of sauce is placed on top of each one. Usually a little cheese, if needed, is sprinkled over the top. It is then up to each person to do their own tossing and dressing. In every case, in Italy all forms of pasta are eaten from a soup plate.

Pasta soups are normally served from the pot straight on to the plates, or from a soup tureen placed on the table. In the case of heavy soups containing pulses, a small jug of good olive oil should be on the table. Those who wish may dribble a little over their soup, which both helps to cool it down and adds a delicious flavor. A bowl of freshly grated cheese should also be available, unless it is a fish soup.

Lasagne, cannelloni and other baked pastas are taken from the oven and placed on a flat serving platter with a folded napkin on it. In this way the ovenproof dish does not slip and it is the platter which is passed around rather than the hot dish. Baked pasta is always allowed to rest for about 5 minutes after leaving the oven so that it has a chance to solidify and settle a little, thus making it easier for each person to help themselves. No cheese is normally offered at the table with baked pasta dishes. If you have a lot of children at your table, however, it may be wiser to serve the pasta on to individual plates in the kitchen and carry these to the table.

ACCOMPANIMENTS

For all those who are old enough, wine should be drunk with pasta at all times. Coffee or tea add absolutely nothing to a plate of *spaghetti*. Likewise, on an informal occasion, always put plenty of bread on the table; it is a compliment to the chef if everybody mops up their sauce with hunks of bread after the pasta has gone.

Almost all pasta dishes contain and are accompanied by cheese in some form or other, except when they contain fish. There are certain very unusual recipes where you are allowed to use cheese and fish with pasta, but these are the exceptions to the rule. Any restaurant where you are offered grated Parmesan with your *Spaghetti alle Vongole* does not know what's what – it is like being served Sauce Tartare with Roast Lamb!

Cheese that is grated and served on pasta is nearly always either Parmesan or *pecorino*. If you cannot get hold of fresh Parmesan it is preferable to use freshly grated Cheddar or Gruyère rather than those sachets or tubs which claim to contain 'freshly grated Parmesan cheese'. They are never fresh and the flavor is mouldy and worlds away from that of real freshly grated Parmesan.

The reasons for serving Parmesan on pasta are twofold; it improves and brings out the flavor of almost any ingredient it is coupled with, and it adds a lovely creamy texture as it melts. Parmesan is the only cheese served to sprinkle on soup. Grated *pecorino* is usually added to dishes with a very piquant, rich flavor.

Never worry about leftover pasta, as it always tastes better the second time around. Toss it quickly in a pan with butter or olive oil until it is heated through, or cover it with Béchamel Sauce and put it in the oven until bubbling and golden brown on top.

Despite the strong views and opinions held in Italy about how pasta should be served and eaten, I must emphasise that pasta should be fun, a food that is to be enjoyed and cooked with flair. It really should not be taken too seriously. Our best dinner parties are those eaten sitting around on the floor with two huge bowls of pasta and one of salad, lots of crusty bread and wine and good company.

BESCAMELLA
Béchamel Sauce

¼ *cup butter*
½ *cup all-purpose flour*
2 *cups milk, cold*

salt and white pepper
pinch of grated nutmeg

Melt the butter in a saucepan until it foams, then add the flour. You *must* wait until the butter is really foaming! Mix together briskly off the heat until you have a really smooth paste, then return to the heat and wait for it to begin bubbling again. As soon as it bubbles pour in the milk and remove from the heat again. Whisk or stir quickly until the ingredients are all blended and you cannot see a single lump. Add a small pinch of salt, a little white pepper and the nutmeg. Stir carefully and bring back to the boil over the heat.

Simmer gently for 15-20 minutes, adding more milk if necessary. Always taste the sauce before you remove it from the heat at the end; if you can still taste flour it means the sauce is not cooked – it will thicken some more and taste much nicer if you let it cook properly. If possible, stir the sauce lovingly until cooked; if not, cover and simmer, stirring as often as you can. Makes 2 cups.

Note: If you make the sauce in advance, take it off the heat when cooked, dot a little butter over the top (or pour over a little melted butter) until the surface is covered with butter. This will prevent the sauce from forming a nasty skin. A very lumpy béchamel can be rescued by whizzing it in a food processor for a minute or so.

"LA POMMAROLA"
Basic Tomato Sauce

This is a good sauce for slimmers, as you can omit the oil or butter and just use the sauce as it is. At about 40 calories per serving, this makes your total intake on a 4oz serving of pasta (360 calories approx.) just 400 calories.

This quantity is for keeping in the refrigerator and using as and when you need it, although kept in this way you should use it up within about a week. In our household I am lucky if this lasts me five days, but if you want a reserve sauce which lasts longer see the recipe for Bottled Tomato Sauce, or freeze this one.

28oz canned or fresh ripe
  tomatoes
1 large carrot, scraped and
  chopped
1 large onion, peeled and
  chopped

2 sticks celery, chopped
1 handful fresh parsley
salt and pepper
2 tablespoons butter or 4
  tablespoons olive oil

Put the tomatoes, carrot, onion, celery and parsley into a saucepan and bring to the boil. Cover and simmer gently for about 40 minutes.

Remove from the heat. Pass through a sieve or food mill and discard all the seeds and mashed vegetables. Pour the pure tomato sauce, flavored in this way, back into the saucepan or put it in the refrigerator until you want to use it.

When you come to using it, season with salt and pepper and add the butter or olive oil just before pouring the sauce on to the pasta. Do not cook the oil or butter, just mix it through. Makes enough sauce to dress pasta for 8 servings.

CONSERVA DI POMODORO CRUDO
Bottled Tomato Sauce

This sauce is made in Italy during the late summer months when the crop of plum-shaped tomatoes is rich and plentiful. All thrifty housewives who enjoy cooking make themselves a supply of bottled tomato sauce to use during the winter. It is essential that the bottles should be dark, so that the light does not affect the contents.

8lb fresh ripe tomatoes

Dip the tomatoes into a pot of boiling water for 10 seconds, then remove and peel. Pass them through a sieve or food mill, then pour the purée into clean, dark bottles. Cap firmly (using a machine such as that for home-made beer), then wrap in paper or cloth and put the bottles into the pot of boiling water (the water must come right up to the cap). Cover and boil carefully for 45 minutes. Remove from the heat and allow to cool completely.

Put the bottles in a cupboard and store until required. Once a bottle has been opened and partially used it should be kept in the refrigerator.

IL SUGO PER LA PASTA
The Sauce for Pasta

This recipe, with rare regional or personal variations, is the pasta sauce made regularly by all Italian housewives and is eaten for lunch, with all different kinds of pasta, about twice a week. The point about *il sugo* is that it should become your own. I have lived in a house where five different women have made it with these very same ingredients, and every single time it was different. If you make it regularly you will develop your own *sugo* too and will know when to make it a bit milder for little children – or more robust for the men.

Overheard on a bus in Milan, where they are notoriously rude about the South: "You can tell she's a Southerner, she puts tomato paste in her *sugo*".

3 tablespoons cooking oil, margarine, butter, olive oil or lard
1 carrot, scraped and finely chopped
1 onion, peeled and finely chopped
1 stick celery, finely chopped
2 tablespoons chopped mixed fresh herbs, or 2 tablespoons
chopped fresh parsley, or ½ teaspoon dried mixed herbs
3 tablespoons tomato paste (optional)
7oz ground meat (literally anything, fresh or leftover, but not usually lamb)
14oz canned tomatoes, drained and puréed or chopped
salt and pepper

Heat the fat and add the carrot, onion, celery and herbs (you can add a clove of crushed garlic if you like). Fry gently until the onion becomes transparent. Add the tomato paste (if used) and mix together, then add the meat. Cook, stirring frequently, for 5-10 minutes. Pour in the tomatoes, stir, season with salt and pepper and cover. Leave to simmer for at least 1 hour – the longer the better. Stir the sauce every so often while it cooks. Makes enough sauce to dress pasta for 4 servings.

IL RAGÙ ALLA BOLOGNESE
Bolognese Ragù

When people refer to things being *alla Bolognese* it means they are served with a *ragù*, of which there are many versions. Here is a simple version of this Bolognese speciality: a meaty tomato sauce, suitable for most types of pasta.

1 carrot, scraped and chopped
1 stick celery, chopped
1 onion, peeled and chopped
1 clove garlic, peeled and chopped
2 tablespoons chopped fresh parsley
2 tablespoons lard or shortening

8oz ground or minced meat (beef, veal, pork, rabbit, or any leftovers you may need to use up)
3 tablespoons butter
14oz canned tomatoes, drained and puréed
salt and pepper
½ teaspoon sugar

If you live in an area where the water is very soft your pasta will come out better than if it was cooked in hard water.

Fry the carrot, celery, onion, garlic and parsley with the lard until the onion is transparent, then add the meat. Brown the meat all over. Add half the butter and the tomatoes. Season with salt and pepper, stir and cover. Leave to simmer for 1 hour, then add the sugar and simmer for a further 30 minutes. Some people add a couple of tablespoons of cream to the sauce just before removing it from the heat and dressing the pasta with it. Makes enough sauce to dress pasta for 4 servings.

BRODO
Basic Stock

Italian saying: "Never leave *spaghetti* on their own while they cook, as they love your company".

The best ingredient to use is a nice scraggy boiling fowl, but for some reason best known to the powers that be, these birds are now becoming very rare. However, a mass produced roasting chicken will do just as well. The point about household stock is that you can use all your leftover bones, carcasses etc. In fact, you must!

Naturally, you don't have to use chicken. Stock can be made quite simply with anything at all, including just vegetables. Remember that this basic stock is not a broth or consommé, which are more elaborate clear soups. Use this stock simply as a cheap and healthy way of flavoring your dishes and especially for soups.

1 chicken carcass
1 carrot, scraped and chopped
1 onion, peeled and quartered
1 handful fresh parsley
1 bouquet garni or handful of mixed fresh herbs
1 potato, peeled and quartered
1 large stick celery, quartered

salt and pepper (preferably rock salt and about 6 whole black peppercorns)
1 tomato, halved
2 cabbage leaves, chopped
any bits of leftover cooked or raw vegetables lurking sadly in the refrigerator
1¾ pints cold water

If you cook pasta at high altitudes it will take longer to cook because the water will boil at a lower temperature.

Put all the ingredients into a large saucepan and cover with cold water. Boil gently for about 2½-3½ hours. Cool, strain, and leave to settle. Remove any fat from the surface and strain into a container to keep in the refrigerator. Use within 3 days.

THE GOLDEN RULES FOR COOKING PASTA

To eat pasta at its very best it is necessary to follow these simple, sensible rules. If you follow them carefully, you should get perfect results every time.

FOR DURUM WHEAT PASTA
(i.e. bought packages of hard dried pasta)
1. Always use an Italian brand of pasta. It cooks, looks and tastes better than other varieties.

2. Allow 3½oz pasta per person. For four people, you will need a large lidded saucepan containing 3 quarts of water. Add 4 teaspoons of salt and bring to the boil.

3. When the water is boiling fast, throw in all the pasta at once. This is the only way to ensure that it cooks evenly. Stir well to prevent sticking, cover the saucepan and bring quickly back to the boil. Once the pasta is in the pot you should never leave it until it is cooked.

4. When the water is boiling again, remove the lid and continue to boil steadily until it is cooked, stirring occasionally.

5. Cooking times: it is impossible to give exact times for cooking dried pasta. *Spaghetti* made by one firm may take 8 minutes, whereas apparently identical *spaghetti* made by another firm will take 15 minutes. Check the instructions on the package and then test a small piece every now and then as it cooks. This is the only way to tell if it is done. Large pasta shapes will obviously take longer than small or thin pasta.

6. To test pasta, pull out one piece and bite it. When cooked, it should be *al dente* ('firm to the bite') but there should be no hard white uncooked central core. Not everyone likes their pasta *al dente* but it should not be so cooked that it begins to lose its shape and fall to pieces.

7. While the pasta is boiling prepare a colander in the sink, a warmed serving dish and a large spoon and fork or two large spoons for dressing and tossing the pasta. It is vital that the pasta is drained, dressed and served as quickly as possible, as there is nothing more disgusting than cold pasta. Also, pasta will continue to cook even after you have drained it, so if you do not transfer it quickly from pot to colander to serving dish and to waiting guests you run the risk of an overcooked mess.

8. As soon as the pasta is cooked, pour it into the colander and shake carefully to drain. Then transfer it quickly to your serving bowl. At this point you can add a pat of butter or dollop of oil, which will add a richness to your pasta but is not advisable if you are trying to lose weight! Carefully mix in your sauce and cheese, if required, and serve at once.

FOR FRESH PASTA
The process of cooking fresh pasta is the same as that for dried pasta but the timing is more difficult and some shapes are more tricky to cook.

COOKING TIMES
The following list of cooking times is approximate and you should test the pasta frequently while cooking:

Type of pasta	Approximate cooking time	
	Fresh	Dried
Thin flat:		
Tagliatelle	4 mins.	10 mins.
Lasagnette	5 mins.	10 mins.
Fettuccine	4 mins.	8 mins.
Tagliarini/ Tagliolini	2 mins.	5 mins.
Capellini	1 min.	4 mins.
Bassotti	1 min.	4 mins.
Linguine	3 mins.	6-7 mins.
Trenette	3 mins.	6-7 mins.
Wide flat:		
Lasagne	4 mins.	8-9 mins.
Pappardelle	5 mins.	10 mins.
Maltagliati	4 mins.	7 mins.
Gasse	4 mins.	—
Picagge	5 mins.	—
Small semolina		
Orecchiette		20-25 mins.
Malloreddus		20-25 mins.
Stuffed		
Ravioli	12 mins.	—
Cappelletti	8 mins.	12 mins.
Tortellini	10 mins.	14 mins.
Tortelloni	12 mins.	16 mins.
Agnolotti	12 mins.	—

Time the pasta from when it has returned to the boil.

Add a little olive oil to the water before boiling to prevent sticking.

Some people throw in a glass of cold water as soon as the pasta is cooked, which is supposed to stop the pasta cooking any further.

If you cook pasta in too little water you will achieve a gluey flavor, not just the wrong consistency.

SOUPS

The concept of pasta as a soup is one of warm comfort on a cold winter's day, for mending a broken heart or for when you're feeling under the weather. Some pasta soups are a meal in themselves, containing enough vegetables and pulses to provide all the vitamins, proteins and carbohydrates you need in one mouthwatering bowl of healthy soup. Others are light and easy to eat, perfect for starting a filling meal.

In certain cases it is important to have a good broth or stock to ensure success. If you do not have a supply of basic household stock in your refrigerator or freezer, just make a quick vegetable broth flavored with lots of herbs.

PIZZOCCHERI DELLA VALTELLINA
Pizzoccheri from the Valtellina

Previous page: *Tortellini in Brodo*

Valtellina is in Lombardy, where it gets very cold indeed. This soup was specially created to warm you all over and is a very economical way of filling you up. It does, however, require you to make your own pasta (see page 154).

¼ cup butter, melted
4 leaves fresh sage, or 3 pinches of
  dried sage
1⅓ cups whole wheat flour
¾ cup all-purpose flour
1 cup milk
1 egg

salt and pepper
3 medium potatoes, peeled and
  thickly sliced
6 large cabbage leaves, roughly
  chopped
4oz Gruyère cheese, thinly sliced

Mix the melted butter with the sage, and set aside.

Make a dough with the two flours, the milk and the egg. Add a little water if necessary. Season with salt and pepper. Knead the dough thoroughly. Roll it out, not too thinly, and cut out your *pizzoccheri* with a sharp knife. They should be about as long and as thick as your index finger.

Place the potatoes and cabbage in a saucepan and add salted water to cover. Bring to the boil and cook for 15 minutes. Add the *pizzoccheri* and allow to boil together quite fast for 3 minutes or until the pasta is just tender but still quite firm. Drain the pasta and vegetables, but keep back some of the cooking water.

Arrange the vegetables and pasta in layers alternating with the slices of cheese in a warmed tureen. Add a little of the reserved cooking water as you go along. At the end pour the sage-flavored butter over the top (remove fresh sage leaves if used) and grind over plenty of black pepper.

TORTELLINI IN BRODO
Tortellini in Broth

In Emilia, the most common stuffed pasta are *cappelletti*, which are traditionally filled with the best parts of a chicken, cheese and ham, and then cooked in broth made from a capon.

As with any 'in broth' recipe it is the quality of the stock which makes the soup. However in this case, the *tortellini* are also very important as their filling must marry well with the flavor of the stock, and they must not on any account be rubbery. This is a typical dish with which to start a Sunday lunch in Italy, as it prepares the palate for the more complicated flavors and rich sauces which will follow. *Tortellini* are sometimes called *cappelletti* (little hats) in certain parts of Italy.

4½ cups good stock
7oz tortellini or cappelletti (fresh,
  dried or home-made, see page
  156)

⅓ cup grated Parmesan cheese

Bring the broth to the boil in a saucepan. Add the *tortellini* gently so that they don't fall apart and lose their filling. The impact of the boiling broth will finally seal them. Allow to cook for 10-15 minutes or until soft. Stir gently from time to time to avoid sticking. Serve at once, with the cheese offered separately for those who wish to add it.

LA PASTINA IN BRODO
Pastina in Broth

Being so warming and so easily digestible, this is perfect food for somebody who is not well, for a small child, for an old person, or as a light starter for a heavy meal. Obviously, the important part of the recipe is the quality of the stock – the better the stock, the better the end result. Some people like more broth and less *pastina* or vice versa. Ask each person as you serve the soup how they like it.

4½ cups good stock
7oz pastina (any shape)

6 tablespoons grated Parmesan
cheese, to serve

Bring the broth to the boil in a large saucepan. When it is really boiling, add the *pastina* by pouring it in from a height of about 6in above the saucepan and stir in thoroughly. Allow the broth to continue to boil for about 10 minutes, or until the *pastina* is well swollen and very soft. Ladle the soup directly into each individual soup bowl or serve it from a large single bowl or tureen if you're being elegant. Serve the cheese separately.

LA MINESTRINA
Little Soup

Every Italian has his own adaptation of *Minestrina*, but it is in fact a standard diet for invalids and babies. It has the same soothing qualities of good rice pudding or any other nursery food and as such is to be eaten in moments of need! Below is the recipe I've used for my son since he was 4 months old.

The Neapolitans often make pasta soups into which leftover packages of pasta are tossed, regardless of shape or size. In this way you get an amusing jumble of different kinds of pasta in your soup, which makes for a pleasant change.

1 onion, peeled and quartered
1 carrot, scraped and chopped
 into 4 pieces
1 large stick celery, chopped into
 4 pieces
1 tomato, quartered
1 zucchini (if available), chopped
 into 4 pieces

1 potato, peeled and chopped into
 4 pieces
1¼ cups water, salted
2oz pastina (my son favors the
 star-shaped pastina)
1 egg, beaten
2 tablespoons grated Parmesan
 cheese

Place all the vegetables and the water in a saucepan and bring to the boil. Allow to cook until the vegetables are very soft. Remove from the heat. Remove and discard the skin of the tomato, the celery and the onion. Mash the remaining vegetables in the hot water. Return to the heat and cook gently until they are well combined. When the soup boils again, toss in the *pastina*, from a height, and stir thoroughly. Allow to cook for about 10 minutes during which time the *pastina* absorbs the soup and swells.

  Meanwhile, in a soup plate, beat the egg with the cheese until you have a smooth frothy mass. Pour the cooked soup over the egg and cheese mixture and stir very quickly so that the hot soup cooks the egg at once. Eat as soon as it is cool enough. Serves 1.

Note: You can, of course, vary this in many ways; for example, omit the egg and use just cheese, or replace the egg and cheese with cooked ground beef, veal or chicken, or even flaked white fish.

MINESTRONE DI ZUCCA GIALLA
Yellow Pumpkin Country Soup

This is a delicious and very filling country-style pasta soup with the added bonus of being a glorious golden color. The pumpkin is in season at the time when one feels the first bite of frosty winter nights and the thought of steaming hot soup is most appealing.

1 tablespoon cooking oil or butter
1 large onion, peeled and
* chopped*
1 large clove garlic, peeled and
* crushed*
2 tablespoons lard, diced
6 cups water

4 medium potatoes, peeled and
* diced*
1lb yellow pumpkin, peeled,
* seeded and diced the same size*
* as the potatoes*
salt and pepper
10oz small cannolicchi
¼ cup grated Parmesan cheese

Never throw away the crust of your Parmesan cheese. Scrape it and wash it carefully and give it to your baby to cut his teeth on. If you don't like that idea, or you don't have a baby, just add it to a soup, where it will add a delicious flavor and soften to a gorgeous chewy consistency.

Heat the oil or butter in a large saucepan. Add the onion, garlic and diced lard, and allow to fry over a gentle heat, adding a little of the water every now and again to be sure the onion cooks and softens without coloring. When the onion is well cooked add the potato and pumpkin cubes. It is most important that they should be about the same size so that they cook in the same length of time. Stir all the ingredients together and add a little more water. Add the rest of the water and stir thoroughly. Season with salt and pepper. Cover with a lid and simmer for 10 minutes.

Add the *cannolicchi* by pouring them in from a height of about 10in. Stir again, cover the saucepan again and allow the soup to finish cooking. The end result should be neither too wet nor too thick, but you can add or reduce the water if you prefer a different consistency. When the *cannolicchi* are tender the soup is ready.

Remove the soup from the heat and let it rest, with the lid on, for about 5 minutes. Transfer it to a soup tureen or individual soup bowls, sprinkle with the cheese and serve very hot. Serves 5-6.

MINESTRONE DI ORECCHIETTE E BROCCOLI
Orecchiette and Broccoli Country Soup

Orecchiette are the pasta which is typical of the Puglia region. They can be bought ready-made of dried durum wheat or semolina. The semolina variety, being much harder, takes longer to cook.

salt and pepper
2lb broccoli, separated into very
* small florets*

1lb orecchiette
4 tablespoons olive oil

Bring two saucepans of salted water to the boil. Add the broccoli to one pan and cook for about 15 minutes or until tender. Add the *orecchiette* to the other pan and cook until just tender. Drain the broccoli well. Drain the *orecchiette*, but keep the water.

Mix the cooked *orecchiette* and broccoli together and add the olive oil. Add about 2 cups of the water reserved from the cooking of the *orecchiette*. Grind plenty of black pepper over the dish, stir it all together thoroughly and serve at once. Serves 6.

Right: (clockwise from top) *Minestrone di Orecchiette e Broccoli; Minestrone alla Genovese; Minestrone di Zucca Gialla*

MINESTRONE ALLA GENOVESE
Genoese Minestrone

Every part of Italy and, indeed, every Italian household or restaurant has its own interpretation of *Minestrone*. It means, literally, big soup; that is, a soup which really fills you up. It can be made as simply or as richly as one likes or can afford – its origins lie in peasant households where all the odds and ends were chucked into a pot to make soup and the pasta was added to give it more body. What makes this a real Genoese *Minestrone* is the *pesto*. Make it fresh if there is fresh basil in season, or else use some ready-made from a jar.

1 cup dried red beans, soaked overnight, boiled very fast for 10 minutes and drained
1 medium cabbage, chopped
3 medium potatoes, peeled and diced
1 large eggplant, chopped
3 large zucchini, diced
8oz shelled peas (fresh, canned or frozen)
8oz green beans (fresh, canned or frozen)

2 tablespoons olive oil
salt and pepper
2 cups water
7oz pastina (medium-sized)
4 cloves garlic, peeled
2 handfuls fresh basil
½ cup grated Parmesan cheese
½ cup grated pecorino cheese
2 tablespoons olive oil

There is much argument as to the truth of the theory that Marco Polo brought pasta to Italy from China. In a document dated 2 February 1279, a certain Genoese nobleman named Ponzio Bastone left to his relatives a barrel full of dried *maccheroni*. In 1279 Marco Polo had not yet returned from his travels.

Place the beans in a large saucepan and cover with fresh cold water. Bring to the boil over a gentle heat and allow them to cook until tender. Add all the other vegetables and the olive oil, and season well with salt and pepper. Cover and allow to simmer for about 1 hour.

Add the measured water and bring back to the boil. Add the pasta by pouring it in from a height. Stir carefully and leave to cook while you prepare the *pesto*.

Pound together the garlic and basil with a little salt. Then stir in the cheeses and thin with the oil. Stir the *pesto* very thoroughly with a wooden spoon until you have a perfectly smooth consistency. All this can also be done with a food processor or blender.

Spoon the *pesto* into the soup as soon as the *pastina* is cooked. Allow the soup to simmer for a further 3 minutes and serve at once.

MINESTRONE DI PASTA E FAGIOLI
Pasta and Bean Country Soup

For this typical Venetian dish it is most important to have a solid saucepan with a very heavy bottom and a close fitting lid. If dried *borlotti* beans are used, these must be soaked overnight and then boiled fiercely for 10 minutes before using.

2½ cups red borlotti or pinto beans	8oz raw pork skin, sliced into thin strips
2 tablespoons olive oil	½ ham bone, best if quite meaty
1 large onion, peeled and chopped	2oz (¼ cup) lard
1 stick cinnamon	salt and pepper
	1lb fresh or dried tagliatelle
	⅓ cup grated Parmesan cheese

Place the beans and olive oil in a saucepan and cover with cold water. Add the onion, cinnamon stick, raw pork skin, ham bone, mashed lard, and plenty of salt and pepper. Put the pan on a very, very low heat and cook for about 2-3 hours, or until the beans have completely fallen apart and made the soup very thick and creamy. Add more water if the mixture seems to be drying out.

Break up the *tagliatelle* into short, stubby sections and toss them into the soup. Stir it all together, and cook until the pasta is tender. Remove the ham bone, pork skin and cinnamon stick. Ladle the soup directly into warm soup bowls and sprinkle a little cheese on top of each one.

With this dish you should also serve a cruet of fresh olive oil which can be dribbled over your soup if you like the flavor of the oil mixing with the pork and beans. Serves 6.

The word *lasagne* is derived from the Greek word *lasanon*. These were among the earliest forms of *tagliatelle*, being long strips of pasta which were fried or roasted and then added to soup or vegetables. The Romans called the same thing *laganum*, and Horace speaks of his delight in returning home to eat his *laganum*.

MINESTRA DI BAVETTE ALLA GENOVESE
Genoese Bavette Soup

In order for this to be strictly traditional, you should use the broth left over after making the famous *Cima alla Genovese*. However, I find it comes out well enough with a good, meaty beef stock, but be sure you can really taste the meat in the stock. The other important ingredient is fresh marjoram, although I have found fresh thyme to be equally pungent and successful.

4 eggs	salt and pepper
6 cups beef stock	handful fresh marjoram or thyme
½ cup grated Parmesan cheese	10oz bavette

Beat the eggs thoroughly with 1 cup of the stock and the cheese, and season well with salt and pepper. Bring the rest of the stock to the boil with the fresh marjoram. Remove the marjoram and throw in the *bavette*. Stir thoroughly. Allow the *bavette* to cook about 12 minutes, then add the egg mixture and whisk thoroughly together. Remove from the heat as soon as the eggs have scrambled and serve at once.

MINESTRONE DI CIPOLLINE
Baby Onion Country Soup

For this recipe you will require those tiny button-sized onions that are served as a vegetable in their own right. If, however, these are difficult to find, I can assure you that pickling onions are just as good. This soup is a real warmer; the best remedy for a cold is to drink a bowlful of this soup and a bottle of rich red wine, then go to bed to sleep it off!

14oz baby onions or pickling
onions
½ cup cooking oil
½ cup drained and puréed
canned tomatoes or tomato

sauce (see page 12), or 2
tablespoons tomato paste
salt and pepper
7oz fine spaghettini
¼ cup grated Parmesan cheese

Put all the onions into a bowl of cold water and remove their skin without taking them out of the water – in this way you will avoid a cry and sore eyes. When they are all peeled, drain them, place in a large saucepan and cover with fresh cold water. Add the oil and tomato purée, sauce or paste, and season with salt and pepper. Cover with a lid and allow to cook gently until the onions are almost completely cooked.

Break the *spaghettini* into short pieces, add them to the almost-cooked onions and stir together thoroughly. Add a little more salt and pepper if you like and let the *spaghettini* cook with the rest of the soup. Add more water if it seems dry and likely to stick.

When the *spaghettini* are tender, remove the pan from the heat and let the soup rest for a few minutes. Transfer it to a tureen or individual bowls, sprinkle with the cheese and serve at once.

MINESTRA DI QUADRUCCI CON I PISELLI
Pea and Bacon Country Soup

Quadrucci are what you make out of the leftover *sfoglia* once you have cut out your pasta. All the little odd bits are kept and cut into tiny squares to be used for soup. You can also buy *quadrucci* ready-made and dried, in which case they will always look much more elegant as they are all even! *Quadrucci* are considered to be a traditional Roman pasta. Once again, for this soup you need some good stock.

4oz thick cut fresh bacon, rinded
and chopped
1 large onion, peeled and
chopped
1 stick celery, chopped

1 sprig fresh parsley, chopped
2 tablespoons butter
4½ cups good stock
1lb shelled peas
1lb quadrucci

Place the chopped bacon, onion, celery, parsley and butter in a large saucepan. Let them all fry together gently until well browned, then add the stock and peas. Stir carefully and bring to the boil. Let cook for about 10 minutes.

When the peas are tender, add the pasta. Cook for 3 minutes if using home-made pasta; dried packet pasta will take longer. The soup is ready as soon as the pasta is tender. Serves 6.

MINESTRA DI PASTA E CECI
Pasta and Chick Pea Country Soup

It is important for this recipe to have good quality chick peas. As with all soups that contain pulses, the combination of pasta with beans, chick peas or lentils makes for an extremely nutritious dish which is rich in precious roughage.

1lb chick peas
salt and pepper
1 small branch fresh rosemary
5 tablespoons olive oil
2 cloves garlic, peeled and
  chopped

3 canned anchovy fillets, drained,
  soaked in milk, rinsed and
  chopped
1 tablespoon tomato paste
10oz small cannolicchi

Soak the chick peas in cold water overnight. The next day drain and place in a saucepan with fresh cold water to cover, a good pinch of salt and the rosemary. Bring to the boil and simmer for 1 hour.

Meanwhile, fry together the oil, garlic and chopped anchovies in another saucepan. Stir in the tomato paste and 1 cup water. Let this mixture cook for about 20 minutes.

Add the chick peas with their cooking water. (They should be quite tender, but still whole.) As soon as the soup comes back to the boil, add the *cannolicchi* from a height of about 6in. Stir in carefully and let the pasta cook for about 15 minutes or until tender. Check for salt, then add a generous amount of freshly ground black pepper and serve at once. Serves 6.

Pasta with chick peas is usually cooked on All Souls Day in memory of the dead. This is one of the most ancient of pasta dishes, a version called *laganum et ciceris* was eaten by the Romans.

QUICK AND EASY
PASTA DISHES

If you come home tired and hungry, a dish of pasta which is quick and easy to make is much more satisfying than most snacks. All these recipes, none of which require great expertise in the kitchen, are really delicious and a great solution to the problem of the busy lives most of us lead today.

Once you have mastered the very simple and basic recipes here you can begin to experiment by combining one or more recipes together or adding your own choice of ingredients. As always, with pasta there are no specific rules. Let your imagination run riot and you will not go far wrong.

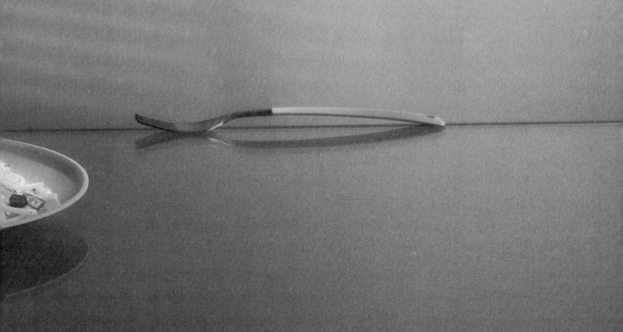

TAGLIATELLE AL SALMONE AFFUMICATO
Tagliatelle with Smoked Salmon

Previous page: *Spaghetti Aglio Oglio e Peperoncino*

This is a well known delicacy, and I here give you my own version. Use fresh home-made *tagliatelle*, if possible, and make them fine and delicate.

1 ¼ cups heavy cream	salt
2 tablespoons brandy	¼ cup butter, melted
¼ teaspoon cayenne pepper	14oz smoked salmon, chopped (a
1 small piece lemon rind, whole	great way of using up all the odd
small pinch of grated nutmeg	scraps from a side of smoked
14oz tagliatelle	salmon)

Heat the cream in the top of a double boiler with the brandy, cayenne, lemon rind and nutmeg.

Cook the *tagliatelle* in plenty of boiling salted water, drain and pour back into the saucepan. Pour over the melted butter and mix together. Add the salmon. Remove the lemon rind from the cream and pour over the pasta. Mix together very gently, pour out on to a serving platter and serve.

LUMACHE CON I GAMBERETTI ALLA PANNA
Lumache with Shrimps and Cream

An elegant but very simple dish for a summer lunch or dinner party. Any small pasta which will scoop up lots of sauce is suitable.

14oz lumache	¼ teaspoon cayenne pepper
salt and pepper	5 tablespoons heavy cream
10oz cooked shelled shrimp	

Cook the *lumache* in plenty of boiling salted water, drain and transfer to a warm bowl. Add the shrimps, cayenne and cream and season with freshly ground black pepper. Toss together and serve very hot.

VERMICELLI CON L'ERBETTA
Vermicelli with Watercress

This very fresh-tasting dish has a strong flavor. A good summer starter.

14oz vermicelli	3oz watercress leaves, finely
salt and pepper	chopped
⅓ cup butter	⅓ cup grated pecorino cheese

Right: (top) *Lumache con i Gamberetti alla Panna;* (bottom) *Tagliatelle al Salmone Affumicato*

Cook the *vermicelli* in plenty of boiling salted water, drain and transfer to a warm bowl. Add the butter, the watercress and the cheese, and season with a little pepper. Toss together quickly and serve at once.

SPAGHETTI AGLIO E OLIO
Spaghetti with Oil and Garlic

If you've been out on the tiles, the experts assure me that in order to wake up in the morning bright-eyed and bushy-tailed, you should consume a large quantity of *Spaghetti ajo ojo* as they are called in Rome, just before you collapse into a drunken stupor. I have no personal experience as to the efficacy of this method, but the recipe is certainly easy enough to make whatever state you're in, and delicious.

14oz spaghetti or spaghettini
salt and pepper
½ cup olive oil

2-5 cloves garlic, peeled or
unpeeled

When cooking *Spaghetti Ajo e Ojo* it is important to remember that it is the olive oil which will carry off the dish. It must be of really good quality, with a strong flavor and smell and a good deep golden or green color.

Cook the *spaghetti* in plenty of boiling salted water. Meanwhile, heat the oil in a small pan with the garlic floating on top. Do not allow the oil to boil or sizzle as this will ruin everything. As soon as the *spaghetti* is done, drain and transfer to a warmed bowl. Pour over the oil (remove and discard the garlic cloves) and distribute evenly with two forks. Grind in black pepper to taste and serve at once.
Variation: if you like a bit of heat, add 1-2 sliced chilies to the oil with the garlic.

PENNE LISCE CON L'ERBA CIPOLLINA E IL BACON
Penne Lisce with Chives and Bacon

Chives have a very special flavor, somewhere between onions and fresh grass. They are easy enough to grow, so you might well have some. The dried variety does not work very well in this recipe.

10 slices bacon
14oz penne lisce (smooth-surfaced penne)
salt and pepper
¼ cup butter

4 tablespoons chopped fresh chives
4 tablespoons grated Parmesan cheese

Fry the bacon, then drain and chop. Keep warm.

Cook the pasta in boiling salted water, drain and put into a warm bowl. Add the bacon, butter, chives and Parmesan. Season with a little pepper. Toss together until the butter has melted, then serve.

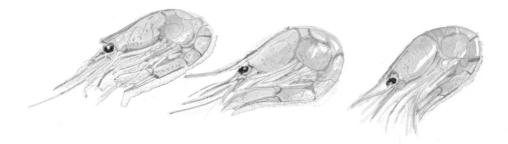

PENNE COL BACON E SPINACI CRUDI
Penne with Raw Spinach and Bacon

This combination of raw spinach with crisp bacon is very popular at the moment and works well with pasta.

8 slices unsmoked bacon
14oz penne
salt
2 tablespoons butter

8oz fresh young green spinach
  leaves, chopped
4 tablespoons grated Parmesan
  cheese

Fry the bacon. Meanwhile, cook the *penne* in plenty of boiling salted water. Drain and transfer to a warm bowl. Add the butter and toss together quickly. Drain the bacon and chop. Add with the spinach to the pasta, toss again, then add the cheese and serve.

FUSILLI COI GAMBERETTI
Fusilli with Shrimp

A very simple and quick dish, you can make it with frozen shrimp at just a moment's notice.

5 tablespoons olive oil
1 clove garlic, peeled
1 chili
6 large raw shrimp in their shells
1lb shelled cooked shrimp

14oz fusilli
salt
2 tablespoons chopped fresh
  parsley

Heat the oil with the garlic and chili, then add the shrimp and toss quickly to cook the large shrimp through.

It was said to be President Jefferson (1743-1826) who first introduced pasta to the U.S. after a visit to Italy.

Cook the *fusilli* in boiling salted water, drain and transfer to a warm bowl. Discard the garlic and chili and pour the shrimp with the oil over the *fusilli*. Toss carefully. Scatter the parsley over the top and serve.

PENNETTE COL BURRO DI TONNO
Pennette with Tuna and Butter

A lovely dish, this requires very little cooking, but you do need a blender or food processor.

¼ cup butter
6½oz canned tuna fish, drained
salt and pepper

14oz pennette
2 tablespoons chopped fresh
  parsley

Process the butter and tuna together to a soft cream in a blender or food processor. Season with salt and pepper.

Toss the *pennette* into boiling salted water, stir to separate and cook until tender. Drain and transfer to a warm bowl. Add the tuna and butter cream, toss together quickly, sprinkle the parsley over the top and serve.

TORTELLONI VERDI ALL'AVOCADO
Green Tortelloni with Avocado

This recipe is very quick to prepare if you buy the *tortelloni* or have a supply in the freezer. If *tortelloni* are not available any small pasta stuffed with *ricotta* cheese and spinach will do. The subtle taste of avocado blends beautifully with the filling of the pasta.

PER PERSON
6-8 green tortelloni filled with
  spinach and ricotta cheese
salt and pepper

½ ripe avocado
⅔ cup light cream
½ cup grated Parmesan cheese

Cook the *tortelloni* in plenty of boiling salted water. Meanwhile, scoop out the flesh of the avocado and mash with the cream. Season lightly with salt and pepper.

    Drain the pasta, transfer to a warm bowl and allow to cool slightly. Carefully blend in the avocado mixture and cheese and serve at once.

CONCHIGLIE CON TARAMASALATA
Conchiglie with Taramasalata

The internationally famous designer Trussardi designed a pasta shape in 1983, so designer pasta is now available in all the best shops!

Taramasalata can be obtained from Greek food stores. A pretty dish for a hot summer day.

14oz conchiglie
salt
4 tablespoons olive oil
8 tablespoons taramasalata

3 tablespoons chopped fresh
  parsley
1 tablespoon chopped fresh mint
  (optional)

Cook the *conchiglie* in plenty of boiling salted water (not too much salt if the taramasalata is salty). Drain and transfer to a warm bowl, pour over the olive oil and toss together quickly. Add the taramasalata and the herbs, toss together to distribute the dressing evenly and serve at once.

ELICHE COL BURRO DI GRANCIO
Eliche with Crab Butter

This dish is very delicate in flavor and pretty in appearance.

6oz fresh or canned crab, drained
  and flaked
¼ cup butter

4 tablespoons heavy cream
salt and pepper
14oz eliche

Process the crab meat with the butter and cream to a smooth sauce in a blender or food processor. Season with salt and pepper.

    Cook the *eliche* in boiling salted water, drain and transfer to a warm bowl. Pour over the crab butter, toss together thoroughly and serve at once.

Right: (clockwise from top)
Tortelloni Verdi all'Avocado;
Eliche in Salsa Cremosa;
Concighlie con Taramasalata

TAGLIATELLE CON SALSICCIA E PANNA
Green Tagliatelle with Sausages and Cream

The *tagliatelle* do not have to be green, but they do look prettier in this dish. Choose mild sausages with a fine texture.

*4 large country (fresh) sausages,
 skin removed*
1 ¼ cups light cream
14oz green tagliatelle

salt and pepper
2 tablespoons butter
½ cup grated Parmesan cheese

Fry the sausages in a pan, breaking them up with a fork as they cook. As soon as they are cooked thoroughly (but not crisp), add the cream. Allow the cream to thicken, then remove from the heat. Leave aside, covered.

Cook the *tagliatelle* in boiling salted water, drain and transfer to a warm bowl. Pour over the sausage and cream sauce and toss together. Add a little freshly ground black pepper, the butter and Parmesan. Toss enough to melt the butter, then serve.

SPAGHETTI CACIO E PEPE
Cheese and Pepper Spaghetti

The four-pronged fork was invented in Naples at the court of King Ferdinand II in order to eat *spaghetti* elegantly.

A strongly flavored dish, this is a favorite among my Roman friends. The secret of success lies in the quality of the *pecorino* cheese and in the generous quantity used.

14oz spaghetti
salt and pepper

1 ¼ cups grated pecorino cheese
1 tablespoon olive oil

Cook the *spaghetti* in plenty of boiling salted water for about 11 minutes, until tender but still quite firm. Drain and pour into a warm bowl. Quickly add the cheese and olive oil, season with pepper, mix together and serve at once.

TAGLIATELLE VERDI IN SALSA CREMOSA
Green Tagliatelle with Ham and Creamy Cheese

I find that Philadelphia cream cheese works best for these quick dishes, but any kind of cream cheese is suitable.

14oz green tagliatelle
salt and pepper
8oz cream cheese, mashed
2 tablespoons light cream

⅓ cup grated Parmesan cheese
3 tablespoons butter
4oz best lean cooked ham,
  chopped in thin strips (julienne)

Cook the *tagliatelle* in plenty of boiling salted water. Meanwhile, mix the cream cheese with the cream and Parmesan, and season with salt and pepper.

Drain the *tagliatelle*, transfer to a warm bowl and add the butter. Toss quickly, then add the cheese sauce and ham, toss again thoroughly and serve at once.

ELICHE IN SALSA CREMOSA
Eliche with Creamy Sauce

Many of the fresh pasta shops sell pasta colored with tomato, spinach, mushroom and even watercress or pumpkin. This recipe specifies multi-colored *eliche*, but it could just as easily be made with any color.

14oz multi-colored eliche
salt and pepper
4oz button mushrooms, sliced
1 clove garlic, peeled and
  chopped
½ cup butter
4oz frozen peas, cooked

4oz prosciutto crudo (Parma, San
  Daniele or similar), chopped
4 tomatoes, peeled, seeded and
  roughly chopped
4 tablespoons plain yogurt
¼ cup grated Parmesan cheese,
  to serve

Cook the pasta in plenty of boiling salted water. Meanwhile, sauté the mushrooms and garlic in the butter for 2-3 minutes. Add the peas, ham and tomatoes and sauté for a further 2 minutes. Season with salt and pepper.

Drain the pasta and transfer to a warmed bowl. Stir in the sauce and the yogurt. Serve at once, with the cheese offered separately.

Giorgetto Guigiaro, a designer well-known for his work for Alfa Romeo and De Lorean, was recently asked to try his hand at inventing a new pasta shape. Giugiaro took the challenge of pasta design as seriously as that of automobile design, only instead of producing a shape which allows air to flow freely over an automobile he produced *marille* (above), a shape whose cavities and ridges combine to trap the maximum amount of sauce.

FARFALLE CON FORMAGGIO E CIPOLLA
Farfalle with Cheese and Onion

You can use almost any cheese for this dish, provided it is nothing too strong; Gouda and Edam are very good.

*1 large onion, peeled and
  chopped
¼ cup butter
14oz farfalle
salt*

*1¾ cups grated Cheddar or other
  cheese
1 tablespoon chopped fresh
  parsley*

Fry the onion until soft in the butter. Cook the *farfalle* in boiling salted water, drain and transfer to a warm bowl. Add the cheese and onion and mix thoroughly. Sprinkle with parsley and serve.

TRULLI CON HUMMUS
Trulli with Hummus

At the beginning of this century, there were almost 300 different shapes of dry factory-made pasta on sale. Today there are about 70. In those days, pasta was sold in plain boxes and it was not considered necessary to "sell" the product with advertising and bright packaging.

Hummus is a delicious appetizer made from crushed chick peas, sesame seeds, oil and garlic. It can be obtained from Middle Eastern food stores.

*14oz trulli
salt and pepper
4 tablespoons best olive oil
6 tablespoons hummus*

*4 tablespoons chopped fresh
  parsley
1 clove garlic, peeled and crushed*

Cook the *trulli* in plenty of boiling salted water. Drain carefully and transfer to a warm bowl. Add the olive oil and toss together. Add the houmous, parsley, garlic, and a generous amount of freshly ground black pepper. Toss together until the houmous is evenly spread among the pasta, then serve without delay.

ZITI COLLA SALSA RUBRA
Ziti with Catsup

This is much nicer than its name suggests! *Ziti* are very long *maccheroni* which you break up to whatever size you require – in this case about 2in long would be suitable.

*14oz ziti
salt and pepper
3 egg yolks
5 tablespoons light cream
5 tablespoons catsup*

*5oz (about 1 cup) chopped cooked
  ham
7oz Emmenthal or Swiss cheese,
  grated
¼ cup butter*

Cook the *ziti* in plenty of boiling salted water. Meanwhile, beat the egg yolks with the cream, catsup, ham and cheese. Season with salt and pepper.

Drain the pasta and put it into a large warm bowl. Pour over the sauce and the butter, toss until all the butter has melted and serve.

Right: (top) *Trulli con Hummus;* (bottom) *Maccheroni con le Zucchine alla Panna*

MACCHERONI CON LE ZUCCHINE ALLA PANNA
Maccheroni with Creamed Zucchini

The traditional way of making *maccheroni* is to wrap a tiny piece of *sfoglia* around a knitting needle, willow branch or similar piece of wood or metal. The rolled-up *maccherone* is then pushed off the end. In some parts of Italy you will still see women sitting on their doorsteps making *maccheroni* in this way with great speed and dexterity. In Basilicata these home-made *maccheroni* are called *miniuch*.

Any kind of tubular pasta is suitable for this sauce, but don't go for anything too big as the dish has a delicate flavor.

3 tablespoons butter
1 onion, peeled and very finely chopped
1 clove garlic, peeled and crushed
4 medium zucchini, cut into thin slices
1 ¼ cups light cream
14oz maccheroni or other smallish tubular pasta
salt and pepper

Melt half the butter in a pan and add the vegetables. Stir carefully, then lower the heat and cover. Simmer until tender. Remove the lid and mix very thoroughly with a fork to break up the zucchini a little. Add the cream and mix together with a wooden spoon. Do not bring back to the boil, just heat through.

Cook the pasta in boiling salted water, drain and transfer to a warmed bowl. Add the rest of the butter and mix together. Pour over the vegetable mixture and toss together. Serve at once, with Parmesan offered separately, if you like.

MALTAGLIATI CON LE LENTICCHIE
Maltagliati with Lentils

If you feel like making the *maltagliati* yourself, the recipe is on page 156, but if you can't be bothered, bought fresh or dried *fettuccine* or *tagliatelle* will do just as well. The lentils must be soaked overnight.

14oz lentils, soaked overnight and drained
2 cloves garlic, peeled and crushed
4 tablespoons olive oil
3 tablespoons chopped fresh parsley
salt and pepper
14oz maltagliati

Boil the lentils briskly in fresh water for 10 minutes. Drain the water away, replace with fresh cold water and bring back to the boil. Simmer gently until soft. Drain.

Purée the lentils with the garlic, oil and parsley in a blender or food processor. Season with salt and pepper.

Cook the pasta in plenty of boiling salted water, drain and transfer to a warm bowl. Pour over the lentil mixture and toss quickly to distribute the sauce evenly. Serve at once.

TORCIGLIONI CON BACON E PISELLI
Torciglioni with Peas and Bacon

Torciglioni work particularly well with this sauce – they get well saturated with the pea and cream combination because of their lovely winding shape. *Eliche* also work very well.

8oz frozen peas
3 tablespoons butter
6 tablespoons heavy cream
salt and pepper

8 pieces lean bacon
14oz torciglioni
⅓ cup grated Parmesan cheese

Cook the peas, drain, then process or sieve to a thick paste. Add the butter and process or blend again. Pour into a bowl, stir in the cream and season with freshly ground black pepper. Set aside. Fry the bacon (not too crisp), then drain and chop. Set aside.

Cook the *torciglioni* in plenty of boiling salted water. Drain and transfer to a warmed serving bowl. Pour over the pea sauce and toss together. Add the pieces of bacon and the Parmesan, toss again and serve.

TAGLIOLINI ALLA NOCE MOSCATA
Tagliolini with Nutmeg

This is a dish which you will like only if you like the flavor of nutmeg! It really depends upon the quality of the *tagliolini* for its success.

1 ¼ cups light cream
½ teaspoon grated nutmeg (more if desired)
14oz tagliolini

salt
3 tablespoons butter, melted
⅓ cup grated Parmesan cheese

Heat the cream with the nutmeg, but do not boil. Cook the *tagliolini* in boiling salted water – they should only take 2 or 3 minutes at the most. Drain and transfer to a warm bowl. Pour over the butter and toss. Pour over the cream and nutmeg and toss again. Sprinkle the cheese over the top and serve.

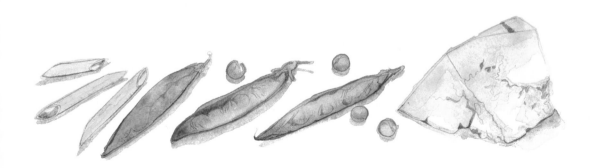

PASTA WITH CHEESE, NUTS AND HERBS

This chapter proves that you can make a delicious pasta dish out of almost any ingredient. All the recipes are good and many are quick and easy to prepare. Where the recipes call for herbs use fresh herbs if you possibly can, or the taste will not be the same, particularly in those which use basil.

Pasta and cheese make good companions; in northern Italy pasta is usually combined with delicate cheese and butter, whilst the southern Italian dishes favour the strong pungent flavor of *pecorino*. Where possible, I have given substitutes which could be used in place of the real Italian cheeses if you cannot find them. For a description of these cheeses, please turn to page 8.

Truffles have now become so expensive that they can only be used on special occasions, but for an idea of their glorious taste try using truffle butter or a can of truffle purée.

GNOCCHI AI QUATTRO FORMAGGI
Four Cheese Gnocchi

Previous page: *Gnocchi ai Quattro Formaggi*

For this dish to be traditionally correct the most important ingredient is the *Fontina* cheese, of which the Italians are rightfully very proud: it is one of the best cheeses there is. However if you can't get hold of it, substitute processed cheese slices. It is a great shame to do this, but nobody will know once you've cooked it. *Gnocchi* here refers to the pasta shape.

2oz mozzarella cheese
2oz Gruyère cheese
2oz Fontina cheese
2oz Edam or Gouda cheese
¼ cup butter

½ tablespoon all-purpose flour
1 cup milk
14oz gnocchi or other short pasta
salt and pepper
¼ cup grated Parmesan cheese

Pasta dressed with butter and Parmesan cheese is also called *all'Inglese* (English style).

Slice all the cheese (except the Parmesan) into thin strips. Set aside. Melt half the butter in a small saucepan. When it is foaming add the flour and stir to a smooth paste. Add the milk, whisk vigorously to remove any lumps and leave to cook for about 10 minutes.

Add the cheese slices and stir until the cheeses have melted and the sauce is smooth. Melt the remaining butter in a separate saucepan and keep both sauce and butter hot.

Cook the *gnocchi* in plenty of boiling salted water until tender. Drain and transfer to a warm bowl, grind over plenty of black pepper and pour over the melted butter. Then pour over the cheese sauce, mix thoroughly and serve, with the Parmesan offered separately.

LE PENNE AL ROSMARINO DELLA BENEDETTA
Benedetta's Rosemary Penne

When Benedetta first made this dish for me, she asked me to guess what the special flavor was. I could not guess at all and was very surprised when she told me it was a huge quantity of chopped fresh rosemary. Try the same trick with your family and see if they can guess. Benedetta says the most important thing is that the rosemary must not cook at all.

1 onion, peeled and chopped
3 tablespoons oil or butter
14oz canned tomatoes, drained
* and puréed, or the same*
* quantity tomato sauce (see page*
* 12)*

salt and pepper
14oz penne or mezze penne
1 tablespoon butter
4 large tablespoons chopped fresh
* rosemary*
⅓ cup grated Parmesan cheese

Fry the onion in the oil (or butter) until transparent, then pour in the toatoes and mix together thoroughly. Add a little salt and pepper and smmer for about 20 minutes.

Cook the pasta in plenty of boiling salted water. When it is almost ready, add the butter, rosemary and 2 tablespoons cheese to the sauce. Mix together and remove from the heat. Drain the *penne*, pour into a warm bowl and add the sauce. Mix carefully. Add the rest of the cheese, mix again and serve.

LASAGNETTE AL MASCARPONE
Lasagnette with Mascarpone

Lasagnette are sometimes called *pappardelle* and in this recipe could be replaced by *linguine* or *tagliatelle*. Most important is the freshness of the *mascarpone*, which can be replaced by full cream cheese, as long as it is very fresh. If you are making the pasta yourself, do this first. You will require 14oz of whatever pasta you choose to cut (see page 155).

14oz home-made lasagnette or	*4 tablespoons olive oil*
similar pasta	*5oz mascarpone or fresh cream*
salt and pepper	*cheese*
2 egg yolks	*¼ cup grated Parmesan cheese*

Cook the pasta in boiling salted water until tender. Meanwhile, beat the egg yolks in the bottom of the serving bowl. Add the olive oil, one drop at a time, and the *mascarpone*, one teaspoon at a time, beating constantly. When the pasta is cooked, drain it and pour it in on top of the sauce. Mix it all up together, add some freshly ground pepper and serve at once, with the Parmesan offered separately.

You can tell if raw fresh pasta is of good quality from the way it looks. It should be shiny and deep yellow.

BAVETTE ALL'ABRUZZESE
Bavette Made in the Abruzzo Style

The Abruzzi are a range of mountains near Rome. In winter when cold winds blow through the Roman streets, people say it must be snowing up there. It is a very beautiful part of the country, and boasts some fabulous traditional dishes. Among them is this one, which uses the yellow flowers from the zucchini or marrow plant which in America are often thrown away.

20-25 zucchini flowers, rinsed	*1 sachet of powdered saffron, or 4*
2 scallions, or 1 small onion,	*saffron threads*
peeled	*½ cup stock, hot*
4 tablespoons cooking oil	*2 egg yolks*
pinch of chili powder	*⅓ cup grated pecorino cheese*
salt and pepper	*14oz bavette*

Chop the flowers with the scallions and fry together gently in the oil. Add the chili powder, and season with salt and freshly ground black pepper. Mix it all together and add the saffron, dissolved or soaked (then removed) in half the stock. Pass this mixture through a food mill or pulp in a food processor. Return to the pan, add the rest of the stock, and cook for 2 more minutes on a low heat.

Remove from the heat and add the egg yolks, one at a time. Whisk thoroughly, then add 1 tablespoon of the *pecorino* and mix together. Leave in a warm place.

Cook the *bavette* in plenty of boiling salted water. Drain and transfer to a warm bowl. Pour over the sauce and mix together. Serve with the rest of the *pecorino* offered separately.

When using fresh basil leaves you should never cut them with a knife as it blackens the leaves and is said to impair the flavor. Instead, tear them apart with your fingers.

LE ORECCHIETTE DI VALENTINA
Valentina's Orecchiette

This is my own recipe and is a favorite with our friends. It is especially nice with the finishing touch of the fresh basil if available, but fresh parsley does just as well. A lovely summer lunch dish.

14oz orecchiette or malloreddus
salt and pepper
½ cup tomato sauce (see pages 12-13)
1 tablespoon butter
14oz fresh cream cheese

10 leaves fresh basil, torn into pieces with your fingers, or 3 tablespoons chopped fresh parsley
¼ cup grated Parmesan cheese

Toss the *orecchiette* into a saucepan of boiling salted water and cook until tender. Meanwhile, heat the tomato sauce. Drain the *orecchiette* and toss them in a bowl with the butter and cheese. Add the tomato sauce and stir very thoroughly together. Add a little ground black pepper and the basil or parsley and mix again. Sprinkle the Parmesan all over the top and serve.

SPAGHETTI AL GORGONZOLA
Spaghetti with Gorgonzola

This dish has a lovely creamy consistency and is a good winter dish. *Gorgonzola* comes from northern Italy where it is used a lot in cooking. In Italy they say the cheese is ripe and ready to use if it has *la goccia* (the drop) – the term is used if the cheese is runny.

14oz spaghetti or any other long thin pasta
salt and white pepper
3oz runny Gorgonzola cheese
2 tablespoons butter

2 tablespoons light or heavy cream
4 leaves fresh sage or ½ teaspoon dried sage

Cook the *spaghetti* in plenty of boiling salted water for about 11 minutes or until tender but still quite firm. Meanwhile, place the cheese, butter, cream and sage in the top of a double boiler. Heat slowly, stirring occasionally. When this sauce has reached a velvety smooth consistency, remove it from the heat but keep warm.

Drain the pasta as soon as it is tender, transfer it to a warm bowl and pour over the sauce. Remove the sage leaves if used. Stir together carefully, add a generous quantity of white pepper and serve at once.

Right: (clockwise from top) *Penne al Mascarpone; Spaghetti al Gorgonzola; Le Orecchiette di Valentina*

SPAGHETTI ALLA SANGIOVANIELLO
Sangiovaniello Spaghetti

A very old recipe from Puglia, this uses olives and capers, and is best if made with fresh ripe tomatoes.

4 canned anchovy fillets, drained, soaked in milk, rinsed and chopped	1lb canned or fresh peeled tomatoes, chopped
4 tablespoons olive oil	14oz spaghetti
2 cloves garlic, peeled and crushed	salt
½ red chili, very finely chopped	15 black olives, 10 stoned and 5 left whole
3 leaves fresh basil, torn into pieces with your fingers	1 tablespoon chopped capers
	2 heaped tablespoons chopped fresh parsley

If you like a sauce with a good flavor but do not like a strong taste of garlic, add a whole unpeeled clove to the sauce while you are making it. But don't forget to remove it before serving!

Put the anchovies into a large saucepan with the olive oil, garlic, chili and basil. Heat, mixing carefully, until the anchovies are creamed, then pour in the tomatoes. Simmer gently for about 15 minutes.

Cook the *spaghetti* in boiling salted water until half-cooked. Drain and transfer to the saucepan with the sauce. Add the stoned olives, capers and parsley. Mix together and finish cooking the *spaghetti*. Transfer to a serving dish, arrange the remaining whole olives on top and serve.

PENNE AL MASCARPONE
Penne with Mascarpone

Mascarpone is like cheese-flavoured clotted cream! It is delicious, but you may have trouble finding it, in which case use the best and freshest full cream cheese you can find.

3 tablespoons butter	3½oz mascarpone, separated into small pieces
14oz lined penne	⅓ cup grated Parmesan cheese
salt and pepper	½ cup cooked chopped ham

Melt the butter in a small saucepan. Set aside. Cook the *penne* in lots of boiling salted water until tender. Pour in ⅔ cup cold water, drain and transfer to a warm bowl. Pour over the melted butter and mix. Grind in a little black pepper and add the *mascarpone* and Parmesan. Mix together, sprinkle the chopped ham all over the top and serve at once.

CANNOLICCHI AL BASILICO
Cannolicchi with Basil

A truly delicious and very easy dish, this is made with *cannolicchi* which, being small and neat, make the finished dish look very pretty. It is a good party dish as it can be easily eaten with a fork or spoon. Best with fresh, very ripe tomatoes.

⅓ cup very finely chopped ham
  fat
2 tablespoons chopped fresh
  parsley
1 clove garlic, peeled and
  chopped
½ tablespoon lard

2lb drained canned or fresh
  tomatoes, seeded and chopped
salt and pepper
14oz cannolicchi
12 leaves fresh basil, torn into
  shreds with your fingers
¼ cup grated Parmesan cheese

Chop the ham fat, parsley, garlic and lard together to create a paste, then fry this gently for about 10 minutes. Add the tomatoes, mix together, season with salt and pepper and simmer for 15 minutes.

Cook the *cannolicchi* in plenty of boiling salted water, drain and transfer to a bowl. Pour over the sauce, add the basil and mix it all up very thoroughly. Sprinkle the cheese over the top and serve.

Note: If you would like to serve this dish cold, leave out the cheese at the end and add 4 tablespoons fresh olive oil instead.

SPAGHETTI ALLA PUTTANESCA
Roman Whore's Spaghetti

The origin of this dish and its name seem buried in a somewhat dim and murky past; some say it was invented by one particular working girl and somebody else told me it was the recipe enjoyed most by the ladies themselves. Yet another person told me that its name is only descriptive – it's a rough and ready concoction . . .

Pasta contains large quantities of Vitamins B and E, which may explain the many stories about the tremendous effect it can have on your sex life, and the myth of the Latin Lover, eater of much pasta!

2 cloves garlic, peeled and
  chopped
4 canned anchovy fillets, drained,
  soaked in milk, rinsed and
  chopped
2 tablespoons olive oil
¼ cup butter
¾ cup black olives, stoned and
  chopped

1 tablespoon capers, coarsely
  chopped
1 tablespoon chopped fresh
  parsley
salt and pepper
7oz canned tomatoes, drained
  and coarsely chopped
14oz spaghetti

Put all the ingredients except the tomatoes and *spaghetti* into a saucepan and fry together gently for 10 minutes. Add the tomatoes and cook over a medium heat for a further 15 minutes.

Cook the *spaghetti* in plenty of boiling salted water, drain and pour into a warmed bowl. Pour the sauce over, mix it all together thoroughly and serve.

Variation: this sauce has quite a strong taste, but to give it more bite many Romans add ½ chili while it is cooking. Don't forget to remove the chili before serving!

TRENETTE AL PESTO
Trenette with Pesto Sauce

There are various slightly differing methods of making the wonderful *Pesto* Sauce. Basil, garlic, pine nuts, olive oil and cheese are a must, but in some places walnuts or a potato are also added. This version of *pesto* accompanies *trenette*, which are fine *tagliatelle* much used in Liguria. If making the *trenette* yourself, you can either make them first and set them aside to dry while you make the *pesto*, or you can make them while the *pesto* is resting. If you want to use a pestle and mortar for the *pesto* in the traditional way, pound the garlic, basil and pine nuts to a pulp, then transfer this into a bowl and continue the preparation by mixing thoroughly with a wooden spoon.

4oz fresh basil leaves
1 tablespoon pine nuts, lightly toasted in the oven
2 cloves garlic, peeled and crushed (more if you prefer a stronger garlic flavor)

3 tablespoons grated Parmesan cheese
3 tablespoons grated pecorino cheese
5 tablespoons olive oil
salt and pepper
14oz fresh trenette

Pesto is only considered to have been correctly made if the basil leaves were taken from a plant which was in flower.

Put the basil leaves, pine nuts and garlic into a blender or food processor and reduce to a pulp. Add a spoonful of cheese, then a spoonful of oil, then cheese, then oil and so on until you have used up all the oil and both cheeses. Keep processing all the time. You should end up with a green cream, with small white flecks in it. Season with salt and pepper and stir in carefully. Transfer the *pesto* to a bowl. Leave it to one side to rest for at least 1 hour.

Cook the *trenette* in plenty of boiling salted water. Take 2 tablespoons of the boiling water to dilute and heat the *pesto*. Drain the pasta, transfer to a warm bowl and pour over three-quarters of the sauce. Mix together. Pour the rest of the sauce over the top and serve. Extra *pecorino* cheese may be offered at the table.

FETTUCCINE ALLA SALVIA
Fettuccine with Sage

A very simple dish, this depends upon the quality of the ingredients used for its success. It is a perfect dish to have as a starter for a dinner party, especially if your second course is intensely flavored. Or it can be a quick supper dish for the family.

½ cup butter
6 fresh sage leaves
14oz fresh fettuccine (yellow)

salt
½ cup grated Parmesan cheese

Right: (top) *Spaghettini Capricciosi;* (bottom) *Trenette al Pesto*

Fry the butter with the sage until brown. Cook the *fettuccine* in boiling salted water, drain and transfer to a warm bowl. Remove the sage leaves and pour the butter over the pasta. Mix together carefully, add half the cheese and mix again. Serve at once, with the rest of the cheese offered separately.

The pride of Piacenza is a type of pasta called *pisarei*, which is made from flour, wet bread and boiling water. For a Piacenza woman to be able to make her *pisarei* really small, so that they absorb most sauce, is considered a great virtue. It is said that in the old days, when a young man introduced his girl to his family in order to gain their approval, her prospective future mother-in-law would check the girl's thumb. If it showed the signs of tiny corns on her skin then it meant she could make *pisarei* and she was a suitable choice.

SPAGHETTINI CAPRICCIOSI
Capricious Spaghettini

To Italian cooks, the term *capricciosi* refers to a dish concocted in a moment of fancy and the result is almost always delightfully different and refreshingly original. It is certainly true of this recipe. But I must add that the most vital ingredients are the fresh herbs, though fresh tarragon can replace the rue. A summer dish, to be served cold, it is very good for parties.

14oz spaghettini
salt and pepper
5 tablespoons good olive oil
2 cloves garlic, peeled and finely crushed
1 teaspoon chopped fresh rue
1 teaspoon chopped fresh spearmint
juice of 1 orange

6 black olives, stoned and chopped
3 canned anchovy fillets, drained, soaked in milk, rinsed and chopped
5 funghi sott'olio (little mushrooms preserved in oil – available in Italian delicatessens), drained and sliced

Cook the *spaghettini* in plenty of boiling salted water. Meanwhile, heat the olive oil with the crushed garlic.

Drain the *spaghettini* carefully and transfer to a cold bowl. Put the herbs and orange juice into the oil, mix together thoroughly and pour over the *spaghettini*. Mix together very carefully to distribute the oil evenly. Add the olives, anchovies and sliced mushrooms and mix it all together. Season with salt and pepper. Chill until required. When ready to serve, stir carefully and add a few tablespoons more of olive oil to moisten.

TAGLIATELLINE CON LA FONDUTA
Fine Tagliatelle with Fondue

This is one of my favorites but again there is the problem of finding the *Fontina* cheese. If you can't, I propose you substitute Emmenthal cheese, a variation which I have tried and enjoyed. The truffle is necessary, but it can be a very small one.

10oz Fontina or Emmenthal cheese, thinly sliced
1 cup milk
2 tablespoons butter

3 egg yolks
14oz tagliatelline
salt and pepper
1 small white truffle

Place the slices of cheese in a bowl and cover with the milk. Leave to soak for at least 2 hours.

In a nonstick pan, melt the butter and add the soaked cheese and half of the milk in which it was soaked. Put over a low heat and whisk thoroughly until creamy. Drop in the egg yolks, one at a time, and beat each one into the sauce very thoroughly.

Cook the *tagliatelline* in plenty of boiling salted water for 3 minutes until tender. Drain and transfer to a warm bowl. Pour over the cheese mixture, stir together carefully, shave the truffle thinly over the top and serve.

VERMICELLI ALLA NAPOLITANA
Neapolitan Vermicelli

A typically colorful, piquant dish from Naples.

4oz dripping
2lb canned tomatoes, drained
and puréed
salt and pepper

14oz vermicelli
¼ cup grated pecorino cheese
¼ cup grated Parmesan cheese

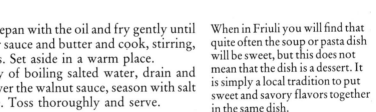

Melt the dripping in a saucepan and add the puréed tomatoes. Season with salt and pepper, stir and leave to simmer for about 30 minutes.
 Cook the *vermicelli* in plenty of boiling salted water until tender. Drain and transfer to a warmed bowl. Pour over the tomato sauce and stir. Add the cheeses, mix together thoroughly and serve at once.

TAGLIATELLE CON LE NOCI
Tagliatelle with Nuts

A very quick and delicious dish, this is best if made with tomato sauce, which you can make and keep in the refrigerator.

14 walnuts, shelled, peeled and
finely chopped
2 tablespoons cooking oil
1 tablespoon tomato paste or 4
tablespoons tomato sauce (see
page 12)

⅓ cup butter
14oz fresh tagliatelle
salt and pepper
6 tablespoons grated Parmesan
cheese

Put the walnuts into a small saucepan with the oil and fry gently until golden. Add the tomato paste or sauce and butter and cook, stirring, over a low heat for 5-6 minutes. Set aside in a warm place.
 Cook the *tagliatelle* in plenty of boiling salted water, drain and transfer to a warm bowl. Pour over the walnut sauce, season with salt and pepper, and add the cheese. Toss thoroughly and serve.

When in Friuli you will find that quite often the soup or pasta dish will be sweet, but this does not mean that the dish is a dessert. It is simply a local tradition to put sweet and savory flavors together in the same dish.

TAGLIARINI AL BURRO CON TARTUFO
Tagliarini with Butter and Truffle

A very simple and sophisticated dish, this shows off the wonders of the truffle! Light fresh *tagliarini* are essential.

14oz fresh tagliarini
salt and white pepper
½ cup butter, melted
¼ teaspoon grated nutmeg

4 tablespoons hot stock
⅓ cup grated Parmesan cheese
1 white truffle, shaved into
slivers

Cook the *tagliarini* in plenty of boiling salted water. Meanwhile, heat the butter with the nutmeg.
 Drain the *tagliarini*, transfer to a warm bowl, pour over the hot stock and add the cheese. Season with white pepper. Mix together, then pour the butter over the top, sprinkle the truffle over that and serve.

PASTA WITH VEGETABLES

It is my belief that, without going to the extreme and declaring yourself a vegetarian, you can do anything with vegetables – and this is more true than ever in the case of vegetables combined with pasta. The original use of pasta as a 'bulk' food, which filled hungry stomachs easily and cheaply, at least in peasant households, was to combine it with vegetables or pulses. Out of those old, simple and traditional recipes have evolved the dishes which we eat and enjoy today.

Most of these recipes can be made from a supply of vegetables kept in the freezer and the contents of your pantry. However, it goes without saying that fresh vegetables are better in every sense, and the fresher the vegetables the better your finished dish will be.

LASAGNETTE AGLI SPINACI
Spinach Lasagnette

Previous page: *Lasagnette agli Spinaci*

If you are a lover of spinach, you'll adore this marvellous, simple recipe which shows off one of the world's best vegetables to its best advantage. You don't need home-made *lasagnette* for this recipe, although you can of course make them at home if you feel like it. For an extra touch of luxury, substitute 2 tablespoons heavy cream for the olive oil and add after the spinach.

2lb fresh or frozen leaf spinach, cooked and squeezed dry	½ cup butter
1 clove garlic, peeled	salt and pepper
3 teaspoons olive oil	⅔ cup grated Parmesan cheese
	14oz lasagnette

Chop the spinach finely with the garlic. Heat the olive oil and butter in a saucepan and add the spinach and garlic. Season with salt and pepper, stir and heat through. Add half the cheese and stir again.

Cook the *lasagnette* in plenty of boiling salted water, drain and transfer to a warm bowl. Add most of the spinach sauce and mix thoroughly. Spread the remaining sauce over the surface, sprinkle the rest of the cheese over the top and serve.

There is a charming folk tale about the invention of *spaghetti*. In the days when all the village bread was baked in a central oven, a young girl was sent down to the village oven one day with bread dough in baskets on the back of a donkey. It was a very hot afternoon and the oven was quite a long way from her home. About half way there, the girl met a young suitor and he convinced her to rest with him in the shade of some trees. While the two young people lay together in a passionate embrace under the trees the poor donkey, with his load, was left standing in the sun. Soon, the dough began to melt in the heat and seep through the cracks and crevices of the baskets, and the hot sun dried it in long thin sticks. So when the maiden eventually got home she produced – not freshly-baked bread – but *spaghetti!*

SPAGHETTI ALLA SALSA DI PEPERONI
Spaghetti with Peperoni Sauce

A delicious sauce, very easy to make and with a lovely sweetish flavor. You can use any color of pepper you wish, although I am told on good authority that the red ones give more depth to the taste.

3 tablespoons cooking oil	2 large peppers, cored, seeded and chopped
¼ cup butter	14oz canned tomatoes, drained and puréed
1 carrot, scraped and chopped	½ teaspoon dried marjoram
1 stick celery, chopped	2 tablespoons white wine
1 large onion, peeled and chopped (preferably a red onion)	salt and pepper
2 cloves garlic, peeled and chopped	14oz spaghetti

Heat the oil and butter, add the carrot, celery, onion and garlic and fry for 15 minutes. Add the peppers and continue to cook for 10 minutes over a medium high heat, stirring occasionally. Add the tomatoes, marjoram and wine and stir together thoroughly. Season with salt and pepper and cook for a further 40 minutes.

Cook the pasta in boiling salted water, drain and transfer to a warm bowl. Add the sauce. Mix together very thoroughly and serve.

SPAGHETTI ALLA SIRACUSANA
Syracuse Spaghetti

The yellow pepper used in this recipe gives the sauce a wonderful golden glow. It looks good enough to eat with your eyes, and could not be more Sicilian.

5 tablespoons olive oil
2 cloves garlic, peeled and chopped
23oz canned tomatoes, drained and roughly chopped
1 tablespoon capers, rinsed and chopped
1 canned anchovy fillet, drained, soaked in milk, rinsed and chopped

1 large yellow pepper (green or red if unavailable), cored, seeded and thinly sliced
salt and pepper
4 leaves fresh basil, torn into pieces with your fingers
14oz spaghetti
½ cup grated pecorino cheese

Heat the oil in a saucepan with the garlic. Add the tomatoes and cook together gently for about 30 minutes. Add the capers, anchovy and yellow pepper and season with salt and pepper. Stir and cook for a further 1 hour. Add the basil at the very end.

Keep the sauce warm while you cook the *spaghetti* in plenty of boiling salted water. Drain and pour into a warm bowl. Add the sauce, mix together, sprinkle the *pecorino* over the top and serve.

A Sicilian saying of the 18th century: "Do you want to live for years and years? Well, drink wine with your *maccheroni!*".

PASTA 'PICCHI PACCHI'
'Picchi Pacchi' Pasta

A very traditional Sicilian dish, this has a superb strong flavor.

2 cloves garlic, peeled and chopped
1 large onion, peeled and chopped
6 leaves fresh basil, torn into pieces with your fingers
4 tablespoons olive oil

4 canned anchovy fillets, drained, soaked in milk, rinsed and chopped
3 large or 6 small ripe tomatoes, peeled, seeded and chopped
14oz spaghetti
salt

Fry the garlic, onion and basil in the olive oil until the onion is transparent. Add the anchovies and mash into the mixture until smooth. Add the tomatoes, lower the heat and simmer for 30 minutes.

Cook the *spaghetti* in plenty of boiling salted water until tender. Drain, mix together with the sauce and serve very hot. No cheese.

In many parts of southern Italy there is an old dish called *Strangulapreti* (strangle the priest). This dish is said to have got its name because it was very popular with priests, who were generally greedy, lusty eaters and would eat so many that they nearly choked to death!

PASTA COI BROCCOLI 'ARRIMINATA'
Pasta with Cauliflower 'Arriminata'

'Arriminata' is a word in Sicilian dialect, from the verb *'arriminarsi'*, which means to move about or, in the case of food, to toss or turn quickly over heat. It applies to this recipe where the finished dish is tossed carefully to distribute all the various ingredients. In Sicily, broccoli means cauliflower.

1 cup olive oil	1 large cauliflower, divided into small florets
3 cloves garlic, peeled and finely sliced	1 tablespoon raisins
2 salted or canned sardines, cleaned and chopped	1 tablespoon pine nuts
2 tablespoons tomato paste, diluted with 3 tablespoons hot water	½ teaspoon powdered saffron
	14oz mezze maniche or other short pasta
salt and pepper	⅓ cup grated pecorino cheese, to serve

The cooking of Calabria is renowned for its use of strong, rich flavors. *Pecorino* cheese is sprinkled over all pasta dishes, which are cooked with sultanas, sardines, garlic, chilis and other vigorous-tasting ingredients.

Heat the olive oil in a very large pan and add the garlic and sardines. Allow the sardines to break up, then stir in the tomato paste and a little pepper. Cover and simmer for 10 minutes. Meanwhile, cook the cauliflower in boiling salted water for 8-10 minutes or until half-cooked. Drain, reserving the cooking water.

Add the cauliflower to the sardine mixture. Stir and simmer, covered, until the cauliflower is completely cooked. Add the raisins, pine nuts and saffron, stir and keep hot.

Cook the pasta in the cauliflower cooking water, but keep it very firm. Drain and transfer to the pan containing the cauliflower and sardine sauce.

Toss the ingredients quickly over a low heat, then remove from the heat, cover and leave to rest for a few minutes. Transfer to a serving dish and serve, with the cheese offered separately.

RIGATONI CON LA ZUCCA
Rigatoni with Pumpkin

Pumpkin is not used a lot in Italian cooking, which is a pity as it has a very distinctive and pleasant flavor. This, however, is a lovely way of using pumpkin with *rigatoni*. Very easy to make.

2lb pumpkin, peeled, seeded and chopped	14oz rigatoni
	salt
4 tablespoons cooking oil	½ teaspoon grated nutmeg
⅓ cup butter	½ grated Parmesan cheese

Right: (clockwise from top) *Penne alla Vesuvio; Pasta coi Broccoli 'Arriminata'; Rigatoni con la Zucca*

Sauté the pumpkin pieces in the oil and half the butter until browned.

Cook the pasta in plenty of boiling salted water, drain it and place in a warm bowl. Add the remaining butter and mix thoroughly. Add the pumpkin, nutmeg and cheese. Mix together and serve.

PENNE ALLA VESUVIO
Vesuvian Penne

Named after the volcano, this dish shows itself to be unmistakably southern Italian by its use of olives and capers. The largest production of Italian capers comes from a group of tiny islands near Naples, in particular the lovely island of Ventottene where caper trees flower in every garden throughout the summer and the capers are harvested in September.

1lb canned tomatoes, drained and chopped
1 clove garlic, peeled
5 leaves fresh basil, torn into pieces with your fingers
salt and pepper
14oz penne
5 tablespoons olive oil

4oz mozzarella cheese, cut into small cubes
12 black olives, stoned and cut in half
2 tablespoons capers, squeezed dry and left whole
1 teaspoon dried oregano

Place the tomatoes in a saucepan with the garlic and basil and simmer gently for about 10 minutes. Remove and discard the garlic. Season with salt and pepper. Remove from the heat and keep hot.

Cook the *penne* in plenty of boiling salted water, drain and put into a warm bowl. Pour over the oil and mix together. Add the tomato sauce, *mozzarella*, olives and capers. Mix it all together very thoroughly, season with salt and pepper, sprinkle the oregano over the top and serve.

Most Neapolitan vegetable sauces have one thing in common; they must all be cooked quickly, so as not to lose the bright red of the tomato.

SPAGHETTINI AL SUGO VACANZA
Spaghettini with Fresh Tomato Sauce

This sauce is very good for those long hot summers when the last thing you want to do is cook. You can prepare it early in the cool of the day, go off to the beach, and when you return just cook the pasta and add the cold sauce. Any pasta will do, but choose one which cooks quickly and doesn't fill the kitchen with heat for too long.

1lb very ripe fresh tomatoes, peeled and chopped
6 tablespoons olive oil
10 leaves fresh basil, torn into pieces with your fingers, or 4 tablespoons chopped fresh

parsley, or a combination of the two
salt and pepper
14oz spaghettini
½ cup grated Parmesan cheese (optional)

In a bowl mix together the tomatoes, olive oil and herbs and season with salt and pepper. Leave the bowl, covered, in a cool place (not the refrigerator) for at least 4 hours.

When ready to eat, bring a large pot of boiling salted water to the boil and throw in the pasta. Stir around to ensure it does not stick together or to the pan. Stir the sauce vigorously so that the tomatoes fall apart. When the pasta is just tender, drain it and return it to the pan. Stir in the sauce quickly as the pasta will lose heat very fast and turn out on to a serving dish. Cheese is not really a suitable companion for this dish, but have your cheese, if you like.

BAVETTE CON LE FAVE FRESCHE
Bavette with Fresh Broad Beans

You need fresh broad beans in their pods for this recipe; once peeled and made into this superb sauce they taste like pure springtime!

3lb fresh broad beans, peeled	*salt and pepper*
5 tablespoons olive oil	*14oz bavette*
3 scallions, chopped	*¼ cup grated Parmesan cheese*
3 tablespoons cold water	

Remove the broad beans from their pods, then gently strip them of their outer skin. Heat the oil in a saucepan with the chopped scallions and add the broad beans and water. Season with salt and pepper, cover and leave to cook for 15 minutes over a lively flame until all the water has been absorbed.

Cook the *bavette* in plenty of boiling salted water. Drain and transfer to a warm bowl. Pour over the broad beans, mix together, add the Parmesan and serve.

ORECCHIETTE CON LE CIME DI RAPA STRASCICATE
Orecchiette with Fried Turnip Greens

This is a traditional dish of the Puglia region and is absolutely wonderful to eat. Be sure the turnip tops are green and tender.

14oz fresh turnip greens	*1 clove garlic, peeled*
salt and pepper	*½ red chili*
5 tablespoons olive oil	*14oz orecchiette*

Throw the turnip greens into a saucepan of boiling salted water and simmer until tender and wilted. Drain, reserving the water in the saucepan, and set aside.

Heat the olive oil in a big frying pan with the garlic and chili. The longer you leave them in the oil the stronger the flavor they will impart. Discard the garlic and chili. Throw in the turnip greens and season with salt and pepper. Stir around and keep hot.

Cook the *orecchiette* in the turnip greens water until tender. Drain and pour into the frying pan with the greens. Stir over a lively heat for a few minutes, transfer to a warm serving bowl and serve.

Puglia has two kinds of pasta which are made without eggs, using flour, water and semolina. The most famous are *orecchiette*, or "little ears", which can be cooked in many different ways and to my mind are the most delicious pasta of all! The other type are *cavatieddi*, which are made by the same method, then rolled on the table top with the point of a knife to resemble little sea shells.

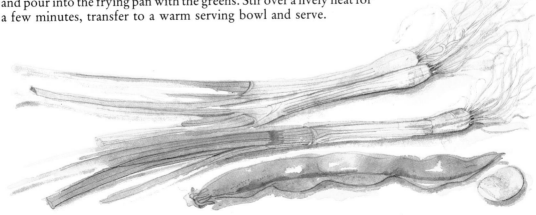

LASAGNE AL SUGO DI FUNGHI
Lasagne with Mushroom Sauce

In this case the *lasagne* are the wide *tagliatelle* with curly edges sometimes called *pappardelle*. This is a succulent treat of a dish, with all the ingredients blending beautifully. It comes from Liguria, where the *porcini* mushrooms grow in the wooded hills in great profusion.

10oz dried funghi porcini or similar dried mushrooms, rinsed, soaked for 20 minutes and drained
1 tablespoon oil
½ onion, peeled and chopped
1 clove garlic, peeled and chopped

4 large fresh tomatoes, peeled, or 6 canned drained tomatoes, squeezed in your hands
salt and pepper
14oz lasagne
⅓ cup butter
⅓ cup grated Parmesan cheese
1 tablespoon chopped fresh parsley

Slice the mushrooms thinly and set aside. Heat the oil in a small saucepan and add the onion, garlic and tomatoes. Mix together carefully and add the mushrooms. Season with salt and pepper and cook for 30 minutes, or until the sauce is creamy.

Cook the lasagne in plenty of boiling salted water. Drain, transfer to a warm bowl, add the butter and stir together. Pour over the sauce and mix together. Sprinkle the Parmesan and parsley over the top and serve.

PENNE E CARCIOFI
Penne with Artichokes

There is a lot of garlic in this recipe so do be sure everyone likes this taste. It goes very well indeed with the flavor of artichokes, as does the fresh mint – another important ingredient for success.

7 fresh globe artichokes, rubbed with lemon juice
4 tablespoons olive oil
3 cloves garlic, peeled and very finely chopped

salt and pepper
2 tablespoons chopped fresh mint
14oz penne
2 tablespoons butter
grated Parmesan, to serve

Remove and discard the tough leaves and the 'chokes' from the artichokes; slice the heart and remaining tender leaves thinly. Put them in a saucepan with the oil and a little water. Add the garlic and season with salt and pepper. Cover and cook very gently until the artichokes are soft. Add the chopped mint and cook for a further 5 minutes.

Meanwhile, cook the *penne* in plenty of boiling salted water until tender. Drain and pour into a serving bowl. Add the butter and mix together, then add the artichokes and stir again. Serve at once, with Parmesan cheese offered separately.

Right: (clockwise from top) *Eliche ai Funghi; Penne e Carciofi; Spaghetti con i Broccoli*

SPAGHETTI CON I BROCCOLI
Spaghetti with Broccoli

This is a spicy hot dish from Puglia. Add more chili if you want to make it really hot.

2lb purple broccoli (green if not available), divided into small florets	*4 tablespoons olive oil*
	2 cloves garlic, peeled
	½ chili, very finely chopped
5 canned anchovy fillets, drained, soaked in milk and rinsed	*14oz spaghetti*
	salt

Cook the broccoli and keep warm. Heat the anchovies with the oil and garlic. Mash the anchovies and garlic into the oil until creamy, then add the chili. Stir carefully, then add the broccoli florets and mix about to cover them with the oil.

Cook the *spaghetti* in plenty of boiling salted water. Drain and transfer to a warm bowl. Pour over the broccoli mixture and mix together. Serve immediately.

ELICHE AI FUNGHI
Eliche with Mushrooms

In Naples they still eat an unusual type of *maccheroni*, which are rather short and thin. These were apparently first introduced into Naples in the 12th century from Sicily where they were the basic food of the many Moslems who lived on the island at that time.

Here, *eliche* are served with a delicious cream and mushroom sauce, which is quite unusual as these pasta shapes are Neapolitan and usually turn up dressed with robust southern-type sauces.

14oz dried funghi porcini or similar dried mushrooms, rinsed, soaked for 20 minutes and drained	*¾ cup heavy or light cream*
	salt and pepper
	14oz eliche
¾ cup butter	*½ cup grated Parmesan cheese*

Slice the mushrooms thinly and cook them for a few minutes over a gentle heat with half the butter and half the cream. Season with salt and pepper and stir, then turn off the heat, but keep as warm as possible.

Cook the pasta in plenty of boiling salted water, drain and transfer to a warm bowl. Add the rest of the cream and butter, the cheese and the mushrooms, mix together and serve.

SPAGHETTI CON 'LA POMMAROLA'
Spaghetti with Classical Tomato Sauce

Just for the record, here is how to prepare the most Italian of all Italian dishes! This is the simplest way to make a tomato sauce for pasta, and it lends itself to many variations. Use any type of pasta you wish.

4 tablespoons olive oil	*14oz spaghetti*
1 large onion, peeled and finely chopped	*5 leaves fresh basil, torn into pieces with your fingers, or 2 tablespoons chopped fresh parsley*
28oz canned tomatoes, drained and puréed	
salt and pepper	

Heat the oil in a small pan and add the onion. Fry until lightly golden. Add the puréed tomatoes and season with salt and pepper. Stir, cover and simmer for about 30-45 minutes.

Cook the *spaghetti* in plenty of boiling salted water for about 11 minutes, until tender. Drain and transfer to a serving dish. Pour over the tomato sauce and stir together. Sprinkle the basil or parsley all over the top and serve piping hot.

The Neapolitans are considered to be the inventors of the simplest, freshest and most delicious tomato sauces in all Italy. They are said to have been the first people in Italy to have used the tomato in cooking, for its bright color as well as its flavor. In this area, where the sun seems to shine more brightly and the colors seem to be more vivid, it is easy to see why they like the shiny red tomato sauces, which have become the most typical mark of their cuisine.

PENNE CON PISELLI E PANNA
Penne with Peas and Cream

A very delicately flavored dish, this is popular as a starter for dinner parties. It is a very easy dish to concoct out of your freezer, with frozen peas and cream; and your pantry where you keep a large supply of packets of pasta!

9oz shelled peas (fresh or frozen)	*¾ cup heavy or light cream*
⅓ cup butter	*14oz penne*
salt and pepper	*½ cup grated Parmesan cheese*

Cook the peas with a little water and half the butter over a low heat. Season with salt and pepper and keep warm. Heat the cream in a small saucepan – do not boil – and keep to one side.

Cook the *penne* in plenty of boiling salted water. Drain and transfer to a warm bowl. Add the rest of the butter and half the Parmesan and stir together. Add the cream and the peas and stir together very thoroughly. Grind in a little black pepper, sprinkle the rest of the cheese over the top and serve.

PASTA E FAGIOLI
Pasta and Beans

A very rich and quite heavy dish which should be eaten in the winter, but is so popular it ends up being made and eaten all year round. The most important ingredient is time – you really must not hurry this dish or the results will disappoint you. It is best if made with home-made pasta.

14oz fresh or dried red beans
⅓ cup lard or bacon fat
1 carrot, scraped and chopped
1 stick celery, chopped
1 large onion, peeled and
  chopped
2 cloves garlic, peeled and
  chopped

3 tablespoons chopped fresh herbs
  (as many and as varied as
  possible, or use dried if you
  must)
3 tablespoons tomato paste
salt and pepper
2 cups hot stock or water
14oz home-made fresh pasta, cut
  into rectangles about 1 ½×3in
  (see page 154)

Pasta e fagioli is the most typical of all the pasta dishes of Venice and the surrounding area. This is due largely to the excellent beans which grow in profusion all over the area.

If using dried beans, soak them overnight. The next day, drain, cover with fresh cold water, bring to the boil and cook fast for 10 minutes. Drain again.

Melt the lard or bacon fat in a heavy-bottomed saucepan and add the carrot, celery, onion, garlic and herbs. Cook until the onion is transparent. Add the tomato paste, season with salt and pepper and moisten with a little of the stock or water. Cook very gently for 30 minutes, adding more stock or water from time to time.

Add the beans and enough liquid just to cover them. Stir carefully and continue cooking for about 2 hours over a very low heat until the beans are falling apart.

Remove half the beans and mash or sieve thoroughly. Return this purée to the pot and stir thoroughly. Add the rest of the stock or water and bring slowly back to the boil. Add the pasta and cook until tender. Stir and serve, traditionally in a terracotta bowl or individual terracotta bowls, with fresh olive oil to pour over the top in small quantities as you eat.

SPAGHETTINI CON SUGO DI MELANZANA
Spaghettini with Eggplant Sauce

The method used for preparing this recipe is exactly like that for a
meat pasta sauce; here the meat is replaced by the chopped eggplant.
It makes a very mellow, smooth sauce.

1 large eggplant, chopped
salt and pepper
1 onion, peeled and chopped
1 carrot, peeled and chopped
1 stick celery, chopped
3 tablespoons butter

2 tablespoons chopped mixed
* fresh herbs*
1lb canned tomatoes, drained
* and puréed, or tomato sauce (see*
* pages 12-13)*
14oz spaghettini
grated Parmesan cheese, to serve

Sprinkle the eggplant with salt and leave to drain for at least 2 hours.
Rinse and pat dry with paper towels.

    Put the onion, carrot and celery into a saucepan with the butter and
herbs and fry gently until the onion is transparent. Add the chopped
eggplant and fry until soft. Add the puréed tomatoes, season with salt
and pepper and cover. Simmer gently for 30 minutes.

    Cook the *spaghettini* in plenty of boiling salted water until tender.
Drain and transfer to a warm bowl. Pour over the sauce, mix together
and serve. Grated Parmesan cheese is an optional extra.

Raw long pasta like *spaghetti* or
bucatini should be springy; if
not, it will be mushy when
cooked.

SPAGHETTINI CON SUGO DI ZUCCHINE
Spaghettini with Zucchini Sauce

The smooth texture of the cooked zucchini is almost like a purée and
dresses the *spaghettini* very thoroughly.

1 onion, peeled and chopped
1 stick celery, chopped
1 carrot, scraped and chopped
3 tablespoons butter
2 tablespoons chopped mixed
* fresh herbs*
5 zucchini, cubed

2 cloves garlic, peeled and
* crushed*
salt and pepper
1lb canned tomatoes, drained
* and puréed, or tomato sauce (see*
* pages 12-13)*
14oz spaghettini
¼ cup grated Parmesan cheese

Fry the onion, celery and carrot together with the butter and herbs in
a saucepan until the onion is transparent. Add the zucchini and garlic
and season with salt and pepper. Cover and simmer for about 5
minutes. Add the puréed tomatoes, cover again and cook for 30
minutes.

    Cook the *spaghettini* in plenty of boiling salted water. Drain and
pour into a warm bowl. Pour over the sauce, mix together carefully,
sprinkle the cheese over the top and serve.

PASTA WITH FISH AND SHELLFISH

Fish and shellfish are plentiful in many parts of Italy and consequently there are many delicious pasta recipes making use of them, ranging from strong, tomato-based sauces with oil and garlic to some superb delicate dishes. Some species of Italian fish are difficult to obtain in this country and, where possible, I have given substitutes, but one which simply cannot be substituted for is *vongole*, those deliciously succulent baby clams. In certain recipes you can use them preserved in brine but in others they really must be fresh and live; the only possible substitute being a similar, very small shellfish.

When making any recipe with mussels, do be sure to follow the cooking instructions carefully. Clean and sort them carefully before cooking and throw out any which do not shut when you tap them. After cooking, throw out any which have not opened. It is just not worth risking the unpleasant results of eating bad shellfish.

SPAGHETTI ALLE VONGOLE
Spaghetti with Baby Clams

Previous page: *Spaghetti alle Vongole*

There are two versions of this famous sauce, one with tomatoes and one without. The sauce with tomatoes can be made with canned clams in brine, whereas the 'white' sauce requires fresh live clams as they are cooked in their shells.

1 ½lb fresh clams or canned clams in their shells	1lb canned tomatoes, drained and puréed
juice of ½ lemon	salt and pepper
4 tablespoons olive oil	3 tablespoons chopped fresh parsley
2 cloves garlic, peeled and very finely chopped	14oz spaghetti

The further south you travel, the more *al dente* the *spaghetti* will be. In Naples they are often eaten still with a dry, hard core in the center and are known as *spaghetti verdi verdi*.

If you are using fresh clams, scrub well, place them in a pot with the lemon juice over a medium heat, cover and wait for them to open. (Discard any that remain closed.) This will take about 8 minutes. Remove them from their shells and if large, slice thinly; set aside. If using canned clams, drain, rinse and remove from their shells.

Heat the oil and add the garlic. Stir and allow to cook gently for 5 minutes. Add the tomatoes and let this sauce reduce by cooking gently for 15-20 minutes. Add freshly ground black pepper and the clams and heat through gently. Add the parsley, adjust for salt and keep warm.

Cook the *spaghetti* in plenty of boiling salted water, drain and transfer to a warm dish. Pour over the sauce, mix together and serve.

VERMICELLI ALLE VONGOLE
Vermicelli with Baby Clams

In this version of the classic dish the clams are left in the shells and no tomatoes are used in the sauce. So you do need fresh, live baby clams. For this version you can use *vermicelli* or *spaghetti*.

3lb fresh clams, well scrubbed	14oz vermicelli or spaghetti
6 tablespoons olive oil	salt and pepper
3 cloves garlic, peeled and chopped	3 tablespoons chopped fresh parsley

Place the clams in a wide pot with 2 tablespoons of the olive oil and cover with a lid. Cook, shaking the pot every couple of minutes to help all the clams open, for about 8 minutes. Discard any clams that have not opened. Drain the clams, strain the liquid and put to one side for later use.

Heat the remaining oil, add the garlic and cook for 5 minutes. Add the clams and mix quickly, then add the liquid left from cooking the clams and bring to the boil. Remove from the heat.

Cook the *vermicelli* in plenty of boiling salted water, drain and transfer to a warm bowl. Add the clam mixture. Stir together, add the parsley and some freshly ground black pepper, mix again and serve very hot.

SPAGHETTINI CON LE SEPPIE
Spaghettini with Squid

In Italy, squid are plentiful, fresh and relatively cheap. I have often been down on the beach at dawn, taking squid from the nets which have been in the sea all night. I have a scar on my right index finger where a squid sunk his beak into me for all he was worth! Outside Italy squid are available frozen, but they are still delicious.

14oz squid, cleaned and
 washed
5 tablespoons olive oil
1 small onion, peeled and
 chopped
1 stick celery, chopped
1 carrot, scraped and chopped

2 tablespoons chopped fresh
 parsley
1 clove garlic, peeled and
 chopped
5 tablespoons dry white wine
salt and pepper
2 cups fish stock
14oz spaghettini

Slice the tentacles on the squid into chunks and thinly slice the bodies into strips. Wash them again and set to one side. Heat the olive oil and toss in the onion, celery, carrot, parsley and garlic. Stir together and simmer for 20 minutes.

Add the squid a little at a time, stirring so that they brown on all sides. Add the wine and cook for 15 minutes or until the squid is tender. Season with salt and pepper and continue to cook, adding a little of the stock every now and then, until the squid is completely cooked.

Cook the *spaghettini* in plenty of boiling salted water, drain and transfer to a warm bowl. Pour over the sauce, mix together thoroughly, add the parsley, mix again and serve.

FARFALLE AL SALMONE
Butterflies with Salmon

Somehow *farfalle* always look very pretty, whatever the sauce. This dish is also delicious and very easy to make from the pantry.

4 tablespoons oil
1 clove garlic, peeled
7 1/2oz canned salmon, drained
 and flaked
14oz canned tomatoes, drained
 and puréed, or tomato sauce (see
 page 12)

1/2 chili, finely chopped
salt
14oz farfalle or similar shaped
 pasta
2 tablespoons chopped fresh
 parsley

Heat the garlic in the oil until the garlic is blond. Discard the garlic. Add the salmon to the oil and stir for a few minutes, then add the tomatoes or sauce and chili. Mix very well, season with salt and simmer for 5 minutes.

Cook the pasta in plenty of boiling salted water, drain and transfer to a warm bowl. Pour over the sauce, add the parsley, mix together and serve at once.

BUCATINI CON COZZE E VONGOLE
Bucatini with Mussels and Clams

Provided you have fresh mussels, it is quite acceptable to use canned clams for this dish. Be sure to throw away the mussels that don't open on their own – you are asking for trouble if you eat a mussel which you have forced open.

2lb fresh clams or canned clams in brine, in their shells	*2 tablespoons meat jelly (from the dripping jar)*
3lb fresh mussels, scrubbed	*14oz bucatini*
4oz dried mushrooms	*salt and pepper*
2 tablespoons cooking oil	

The very first pasta shapes to have a name were called *trii* in parts of Italy most influenced by Arab culture. The word *trii* is derived from the Arab word *itryia* which means a string of pasta with a hole down the centre, just like *bucatini*.

If using fresh clams, scrub them well. Cook the mussels and clams in a large frying pan until they open (discard any that remain closed). Remove from the shells and set aside. If using canned clams, drain, rinse and remove from their shells.

Soak the dried mushrooms in warm water for 20 minutes. Drain. Put them in a small pan with the oil and meat jelly and cook for about 10 minutes over a low heat, adding a little water if dry.

Place the mussels, clams and mushrooms in a large saucepan and mix all together. If using canned clams, add at this point. Keep warm.

Cook the *bucatini* in plenty of boiling salted water, drain and transfer to a warm bowl. Pour over the sauce, add some freshly ground black pepper, mix all together and serve.

PAPPARDELLE CON IL GRANCHIO
Pappardelle with Crab

If you are lucky enough to have fresh crab for this recipe it will be that much better, but a can of crab will do just as well once it is combined with all the other ingredients. A sophisticated dish, this is good for dinner parties but very simple to make. Fresh *pappardelle* are best, but use dried for speed and simplicity.

1 cup butter	*salt*
14oz crabmeat, cleaned and flaked	*½ teaspoon cayenne pepper*
3 tablespoons brandy or white wine	*14oz pappardelle*
	2 tablespoons chopped fresh parsley
¾ cup heavy or light cream	

Melt half the butter over a very gentle heat and add the crab. Stir together carefully, then add the brandy or wine and raise the heat to evaporate the alcohol. Pour in the cream and mix with care. Season with salt and cayenne pepper, stir and cook for a further 2 minutes on minimum heat. Keep warm.

Cook the *pappardelle* in plenty of boiling salted water, drain and transfer to a warm bowl. Add the remaining butter and mix together quickly. Pour the pasta on to a serving platter, spread out flat and pour the hot crab sauce all over the top. Sprinkle the parsley over and serve.

Right: (clockwise from top) *Bucatini con Cozze e Vongole; Farfalle al Salmone; Pappardelle con il Granchio*

SPAGHETTI ALLA CARRETTIERA
Spaghetti with Carrettiera Sauce

The following list of ingredients may appear rather strange to you, but trust me. This is a relatively modern recipe, but nonetheless well tried and tested.

1 clove garlic, peeled and crushed
3oz fresh bacon, chopped
5 tablespoons olive oil
10oz dried or fresh funghi porcini
or similar dried mushrooms,
soaked for 20 minutes, drained
and thinly sliced

1 tablespoon meat jelly (from the
bottom of a dripping jar, see
page 7), dissolved in 2
tablespoons hot water
salt and pepper
14oz spaghetti
6½oz canned tuna fish, drained
and flaked
⅓ cup grated Parmesan cheese

Place the garlic, chopped bacon and olive oil in a saucepan over a medium heat. Allow the fat on the chopped bacon to become transparent, then add the mushrooms and the dissolved meat jelly. Season with salt and pepper and stir. Allow to cook for about 15 minutes.

Cook the *spaghetti* in plenty of boiling salted water, drain and transfer to a warm bowl. Add the tuna to the sauce, heat through very quickly over a high heat, then pour over the pasta. Mix together, sprinkle the cheese over the top and serve at once.

SPAGHETTI ALLA TARANTINA
Spaghetti Tarantina Style

Nothing in Sicilian cooking is considered as important as their superb pasta dishes, which are dressed in a thousand different ways but seldom using either meat or cheese. Sicilian pasta has a flavor all of its own, due, so they say, to the grain used, which is different from that of the mainland.

This is a dish from Taranto, in Sicily. It has a real taste of the sea and calls for fresh eels, which may be replaced by mackerel should eel prove difficult to obtain.

10oz clams (fresh or canned in
brine), in their shells if possible
10oz mussels (fresh, frozen or
canned in brine), in their shells
if possible
4 tablespoons dry white wine
6 tablespoons olive oil
2 cloves garlic, peeled and
crushed
7oz shelled shrimp

7oz eel or mackerel fillet, cleaned
and cut into cubes
10oz canned tomatoes, drained
and puréed
salt and pepper
4 large scallops
3 tablespoons chopped fresh
parsley
14oz spaghetti

If using fresh clams and mussels scrub them well, then steam with the wine over a medium heat until they open. Discard any that remain closed. Remove them from the pan and take most of them out of their shells; keep a few of the better looking ones in their shells to garnish the finished dish at the end. Set aside. Let the cooking liquor and that from the shells settle, then strain it carefully through a very fine sieve and set aside. If using canned clams or mussels, drain, rinse and remove from their shells.

Heat the olive oil with the garlic in a large saucepan. Add the shrimps, then the shelled mussels and clams with their liquor and the eel or mackerel. Stir together for a few minutes, then add the tomatoes. Season with salt and pepper, cover and simmer for 20 minutes. Add a little water occasionally if the sauce appears to be drying out. Just before you remove the sauce from the heat, add the scallops and parsley. Stir together and keep warm.

Cook the *spaghetti* in plenty of boiling salted water, drain and transfer to a warm bowl. Pour over the sauce, mix together and serve, garnished with the mussels and/or clams you left in the shell. Make sure that each person has a scallop in the center of his portion.

MACCHERONCELLI ALLA CALABRESE
Maccheroncelli Calabrese Style

Calabria is an area of southern Italy where they use golden raisins a lot in the preparation of pasta.

Breadcrumbs fried to a deep gold in olive oil are used as a substitute for Parmesan in many pasta dishes all over southern Italy, where many people are too poor to use Parmesan.

1lb fresh or frozen sardines (not canned), cleaned
4 tablespoons olive oil
2 cloves garlic, peeled and crushed
1 tablespoon golden raisins, soaked in cold water to swell
1 tablespoon chopped fresh parsley
1 tablespoon dried breadcrumbs
salt and pepper
14oz maccheroncelli

Toss the sardines into a little boiling water and half cook them. Drain. Heat the olive oil with the garlic and add the sardines, raisins, parsley and breadcrumbs. Stir together over a medium heat until the sardines are completely cooked. Season with salt and pepper, and keep warm.

Cook the *maccheroncelli* in plenty of boiling salted water, drain and transfer to a warm bowl. Pour over the hot sauce, mix together and serve at once.

LINGUINE TUTTO MARE
All Sea Linguine

I don't think the name given to this dish is quite accurate as it contains button mushrooms. However, it is absolutely delicious – quite hot and spicy. Choose whatever seafood you prefer, though it is important to have the squid.

1lb assorted seafood (including squid, shrimp and mussels), cleaned and shelled if necessary
6 tablespoons olive oil
1 cup dry white wine
14oz canned tomatoes, puréed
½ chili, chopped
salt and pepper

4oz button mushrooms, thinly sliced
1 small carrot, scraped and chopped
1 small onion, peeled and chopped
2 tablespoons chopped fresh parsley
14oz linguine

There are recipes written in Roman times which call for strips of pasta deep-fried in boiling oil and then dressed with *garum*, a liqueur made from fish gut which the Romans were fond of putting in many of their dishes.

Prepare all the seafood and set it to one side in separate piles. Heat half the olive oil and toss in the squid. Brown gently, then raise the heat and add half the wine. Allow the wine to evaporate, then lower the heat and add the tomatoes, chili and a little salt. Simmer for 30 minutes or until the squid is tender. Add the mushrooms and cook for a further 15 minutes.

Meanwhile, in another pan, heat the rest of the oil with the carrot and onion and fry until the onion is transparent. Add the remaining seafood, pour over the remaining wine and cook together over high heat for 5-10 minutes. Season with salt and pepper. Add half the parsley to each sauce and remove from the heat.

Cook the linguine in plenty of boiling salted water, drain and transfer to a warm bowl. Pour over the two sauces, mix together and serve hot.

SPAGHETTINI AL CAVIALE
Spaghettini with Caviar

Obviously the better the caviar the better this dish will be, but it seems a shame to use something as expensive as Beluga for a dish like this: better to eat it as it is intended to be eaten – but that's quite another story!

14oz spaghettini or vermicelli
salt
½ cup unsalted butter

1oz caviar (the contents of a small glass jar)

Right: *Linguine Tutto Mare*

Cook the pasta in plenty of boiling salted water, drain, reserving a little cooking water and pour back into the saucepan. Add the butter and mix together, then add the caviar and mix again. Moisten with the reserved cooking water, transfer to a serving dish and serve.

LINGUINE DEL GHIOTTONE
Greedy Linguine

A really simple and quick recipe, you can make this out of the pantry.
Use any pasta you like in place of the *linguine*.

14oz linguine
salt and pepper
5 tablespoons olive oil
2 garlic cloves, peeled and
 crushed
½ cup capers

⅔ cup olives, preferably black,
 stoned and cut into quarters
1 tablespoon chopped fresh
 parsley
4oz canned tuna fish, drained
 and flaked

Cook the pasta in plenty of boiling salted water. Meanwhile, heat the
olive oil with the garlic. When the garlic is just blond, add the capers,
olives and half the parsley and season with salt and pepper. Add 1
tablespoon of hot water from the pasta pot. Let the sauce simmer for
a couple of minutes, then add the tuna and mix well. Remove from
the heat.

Drain the pasta, dress with the sauce and serve.

FETTUCCINE ALL'ARAGOSTA
Fettuccine with Lobster

Frozen whole lobster is now widely available; it is much cheaper than fresh and in this recipe works very well. Fresh lobster should be eaten by itself as a treat in my opinion, but if you feel extravagant use it for this terrific dish! Fresh *fettuccine*, please.

1 cup broth in which the lobster was boiled, strained, or fish stock	*salt and white pepper*
1 cup dry white wine	*meat from 2 medium cooked lobsters, broken up*
1 cup heavy or light cream	*14oz fettuccine*
1 shallot, very finely chopped	*2 tablespoons chopped fresh parsley*
¼ cup butter	

In a small saucepan, heat the lobster broth or fish stock with the white wine and boil gently to reduce by about one-third. Add the cream, lower the heat and simmer very gently, stirring constantly, for 2 minutes. Remove from the heat.

Fry the shallot in half the butter until transparent, then add to the cream sauce. Season with salt and white pepper, then add the lobster meat and mix together very gently. Keep warm.

Cook the *fettuccine* in plenty of boiling salted water, drain and transfer to a warm bowl. Add the remaining butter and mix together, then add half the lobster sauce and mix again with care. Turn out on to a serving platter, pour over the rest of the sauce, sprinkle over the parsley and serve with a flourish.

The most serious thing that can happen to factory and home-made pasta is *la botta*, which means that it catches a sudden chill while drying. This will cause it to fall apart when you cook it. Before there were pasta factories with drying plants, pasta was made by local artisans all over Italy and many different kinds of drying rack were invented to dry large amounts of pasta safely out of doors. In Friuli, where the climate is unsuitable for drying pasta outdoors, they invented a kind of windmill for the purpose. You can still see pasta left outside houses to dry in the area near Gragano.

TAGLIATELLE CON LE ACCIUGHE E IL TONNO
Tagliatelle with Anchovies and Tuna Fish

This recipe is very unusual in that it calls for grated Parmesan cheese. The dish depends on the quality of the tuna, so buy the best you can afford and this dish will be fit for any king. Use fresh or dried pasta so long as it isn't green.

¼ cup butter	*1 tablespoon chopped fresh parsley*
2 tablespoons oil	*salt and pepper*
4oz best quality canned tuna fish, drained and very finely chopped	*14oz tagliatelle*
3 canned anchovy fillets, drained, soaked in milk, rinsed and very finely chopped	*¼ cup grated Parmesan cheese*

Heat the butter and oil in a pan and add the tuna and anchovies. Mix together very thoroughly. Fry gently for no more than 3 minutes, then add the chopped parsley and season with salt and pepper. Remove from the heat and keep warm.

Cook the *tagliatelle* in plenty of boiling salted water, drain and transfer to a warm bowl. Pour over the sauce, add the cheese, mix together thoroughly and serve.

PENNE CON IL TONNO E LE OLIVE NERE
Penne with Tuna Fish and Black Olives

This is a very simple recipe. You can leave out the olives if you do not like them; the dish is still delicious and can be made at a moment's notice out of the pantry.

4 tablespoons olive oil
1 onion, peeled and chopped
2 cloves garlic, peeled and
  chopped
15 black olives, stoned
14oz canned tomatoes, drained
  and chopped

pinch of dried herbs
6½oz canned tuna fish, drained
  and flaked
salt and pepper
14oz penne

Heat the olive oil in a pan and add the onion, garlic and olives. Cook until the onion is transparent, then add the tomatoes and stir vigorously together. Simmer for 15 minutes. Add the herbs and tuna fish, stir and season with salt and pepper. Leave to simmer for a further 5 minutes.

Meanwhile, cook the pasta in the boiling salted water, drain and transfer to a warm bowl. Pour over the sauce, mix together and serve.

TAGLIATELLE VERDI ALLA MARINARA
Green Tagliatelle with Mussels

A proverb from Emilia: "Let the *tagliatelle* be long, but may the bills be very short".

This is a very pretty dish and is unusual in that green pasta is not often served with fish. I find that fresh green *tagliatelle* makes the dish too heavy for my taste, so I always use the dried sort, but feel free to try it out with fresh *tagliatelle*. It is best if the mussels are fresh, of course.

2lb fresh mussels, scrubbed and
  'bearded'
5 tablespoons olive oil
½ onion, peeled and chopped
1 clove garlic, peeled and crushed

6 canned tomatoes, drained and
  puréed
2 tablespoons chopped fresh
  parsley
salt and pepper
14oz green tagliatelle

Place the mussels in a pan with 2 tablespoons of the oil and heat, shaking the pan to help the mussels open. After 10-15 minutes, remove from the heat. Take out some of the best looking mussels and put to one side in their shells for garnishing at the end. Remove the remaining mussels from their shells and set aside. Allow the cooking liquor and liquor from the shells to settle, then strain through a very fine sieve and put aside.

Heat the remaining oil with the onion and the garlic and cook until the onion becomes transparent. Add the tomatoes and parsley and cook briskly together for 15 minutes. Add the mussels and a little of their cooking liquor (3-4 tablespoons) and stir together gently. Season with salt and pepper. Heat through, then remove from heat.

Cook the *tagliatelle* in boiling salted water, drain and transfer to a bowl. Mix in the sauce, turn out on to a serving platter, arrange the reserved mussels in their shells on top and serve.

Right: (top) *Penne con il Tonno e le Olive Nere; Tagliatelle Verdi alla Marinara*

PASTA WITH POULTRY AND GAME

◆———————————————

There are not very many recipes for pasta with poultry and game because on the whole Italians do not eat much poultry and game is often used with other accompaniments such as *polenta*. It may seem odd that chicken is used so seldom, but Italians prefer to eat a bird which has been left free to roam and peck where it will, rather than consume a factory-reared chicken which has suffered in a battery system. It goes without saying that 'free' chickens taste much nicer than battery chickens.

As most people know, the Italian idea of game is quite different from the American and British version. Until quite recently, the shooting season in Italy meant that virtually anything which so much as quivered got shot, including, to my horror, swallows! This led to a variety of birds and animals being served up in dishes under the dubious heading of 'game'. However, some restrictions and regulations have now been put into operation and they appear to be working, judging by the increased number of birds you now see in the country.

PAPPARDELLE ALLA LEPRE
Pappardelle with Hare

Previous page: Pappardelle alla Lepre

When there is no hare around, I use rabbit for this recipe, particularly if it's a stringy old jack rabbit that will need a lot of cooking. If you can get hold of the kidneys, do keep and use them, as they definitely improve the dish. Fresh *pappardelle* should really be used.

1 tablespoon chopped fresh herbs (including parsley, thyme, rosemary) or 1 teaspoon mixed dried herbs	the kidneys, cleaned and cut in half
1 carrot, scraped and chopped	22oz canned tomatoes, drained and puréed
1 onion, peeled and chopped	2 tablespoons tomato paste
1 stick celery, chopped	2 cups stock
1/4 cup butter	salt and pepper
1 hare or rabbit, cut into pieces	14oz fresh pappardelle (see page 155)
	grated Parmesan cheese, to serve

Pappardelle alla Lepre is the great speciality of the city of Arezzo. In that city they also use the head of the hare for the dish.

Place the herbs and vegetables in a large flameproof casserole with the butter and fry gently until the onion is transparent. Add the meat and brown the joints all over, then add the kidneys. Pour in the tomatoes, mix together thoroughly, then add the tomato paste and stock. Season with salt and pepper, cover and leave to simmer for about 3 hours.

Remove the meat and set aside to serve as a second course. Mix the sauce very thoroughly, check the seasoning and set aside in a warm place.

Cook the *pappardelle* in plenty of boiling salted water, drain and transfer to a warm bowl. Pour over the sauce, mix together very thoroughly and serve with freshly grated Parmesan cheese offered separately.

Note: The hare is sometimes served with the pasta – it is laid on top of the dressed *pappardelle* and you eat the whole thing together.

TAGLIATELLE COL POLLO
Tagliatelle with Chicken

Here the chicken can be served as a second course to the meal, with a delicious pasta dish as an excellent starter. Use a nice, tender young chicken, and get the butcher to cut it into pieces, or buy chicken quarters.

1 large onion, peeled and chopped	1 cup milk
4 tablespoons olive oil	salt and pepper
1/3 cup butter	2 tablespoons tomato paste, diluted with 4 tablespoons hot water
1 chicken, jointed	
5 tablespoons dry red wine	14oz fresh tagliatelle
1 teaspoon meat jelly (from the dripping jar)	1/3 cup grated Parmesan cheese

Fry the onion gently in the oil and butter until it is transparent. Lay the pieces of chicken on top of the onion, and brown them carefully on all sides. Add the wine and raise the heat to evaporate the alcohol. Whisk the meat jelly into the milk and add to the pot. Season with salt and pepper, lower the flame, and leave to simmer very gently for 15 minutes.

Add the diluted tomato paste and allow the chicken to finish cooking very, very gently, adding a little hot water every so often to avoid drying out. When the chicken is cooked, remove it and set it aside. Stir the sauce carefully; it should be quite thick, and there should be enough of it to dress the *tagliatelle* thoroughly.

Cook the pasta in plenty of boiling salted water, drain and transfer to a warm bowl. Pour over the sauce, toss together and serve, with the cheese offered separately.

BIGOLI CON L'ANATRA
Bigoli with Duck

The sauce here is absolutely superb, so if you are like me and don't like whole wheat pasta, try the sauce with some other kind, like some nice fresh *tagliatelle all'uovo*. For a less fatty dish, skin the duck before boiling it.

In the Venice area *bigoli* are always made with whole wheat flour and fashioned with a tool called a *torchietto*. In the Mantua area *bigoli* are simply rather thick, home-made *spaghetti* made with plain flour. The people of Mantua say "I'm going for some *bigoli*", meaning that they are going out for a good meal.

1 young duckling (including all the giblets)	*salt and pepper*
	¼ cup butter
1 large onion, peeled	*pinch of dried sage*
1 large carrot, scraped	*14oz bigoli*
1 stick celery	*¼ cup grated Parmesan cheese*

Put the duckling in a large saucepan with the onion, carrot and celery, and season with salt and pepper. Simmer for about 1 hour, or until cooked. Meanwhile, chop the liver and other giblets of the duck. Melt the butter with the sage until foaming, add the giblets and season with salt and pepper. Cook gently, adding a little boiling broth from the pot in which the duck is cooking.

Remove the duck and vegetables from the broth. Set the duck aside to be served as a second course to the meal. Chop the vegetables and put them in the pan with the duck giblets. Add a little more of the broth to moisten thoroughly.

Cook the pasta in the duck's broth, drain and transfer to a warm bowl. Pour over the sauce and mix together very carefully. Add the Parmesan cheese, mix once more and serve.

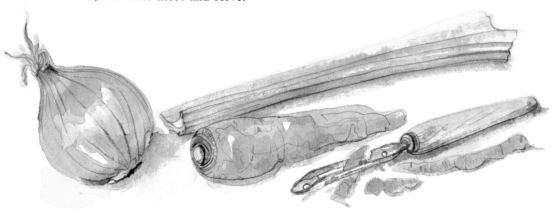

LASAGNE ALLA CACCIATORA CON POLLO
Huntsman's Lasagne with Chicken

For this recipe, you can either make Genoese *picagge* (page 155) or cut ordinary big *lasagne* in half. Alternatively you can use *pappardelle*. The pasta can be green or yellow, depending on which you prefer and what is available. Vary the recipe by using rabbit instead of chicken.

1 onion, peeled and chopped
2 cloves garlic, peeled and chopped
5 tablespoons cooking oil
1 chicken, cut into 8 pieces
4oz bacon, chopped
5 tablespoons Marsala

2lb drained canned or fresh, ripe tomatoes, chopped
salt and pepper
14oz fresh green or yellow lasagne
⅓ cup grated Parmesan cheese

On 19 March, the Feast of St Joseph, the people of Lucania make vast quantities of home-made flour and water *lasagne* to distribute to the really poor people of their region.

Fry the onion and garlic in the oil, then add the chicken pieces and bacon and brown the chicken carefully. Add the Marsala and allow the alcoholic fumes to evaporate. Add the tomatoes. Season with salt and pepper, stir and cover. Allow to simmer for about 30 minutes, stirring occasionally.

Cook the pasta in plenty of boiling salted water, drain and transfer to a warm bowl. Pour over three-quarters of the sauce, mix together, add half the Parmesan and mix again. Arrange the chicken on top, pour over the rest of the sauce, sprinkle the remaining cheese over the top and serve.

VERMICELLI DI GALA
Vermicelli for a Special Occasion

I suppose this recipe should be among the recipes in the chapter entitled Party Pieces, but it is more fun than a fancy dish. It is also a very good way of using up leftover chicken or turkey.

14oz vermicelli
salt and pepper
2 tablespoons meat jelly (from the dripping jar), or gravy
3 tablespoons butter
⅓ cup grated Parmesan cheese
7oz cooked chicken or turkey meat (preferably breast), thinly sliced

4oz cooked tongue, cut into thin strips
7oz hot cooked peas
7oz mozzarella cheese, thinly sliced
3 ripe tomatoes, sliced and lightly fried in butter
1 small truffle (optional)

Cook the *vermicelli* in plenty of boiling salted water, drain and pour back into the saucepan. Add the meat extract or gravy, butter, half the Parmesan, a few pieces of chicken or turkey, a few pieces of tongue, half the peas and a little salt and pepper. Mix it all together. Arrange the pasta mixture on an ovenproof platter in a pyramid shape. Arrange the remaining ingredients all over the sides, including the slices of *mozzarella* and tomatoes. Shave the truffle (if used) over the finished work of art, and place in a preheated 425° oven. Cook for 5 minutes. Sprinkle the rest of the Parmesan over the top and serve.

Right: (top) *Tajarin con i Fegatini di Pollo;* (bottom) *Lasagne alla Cacciatora con Pollo*

TAJARIN CON I FEGATINI DI POLLO
Tajarin with Chicken Livers

Tajarin are fine *tagliatelle* as made in Piedmont. The dish is delicious and very quick and easy to make. Do not overcook the chicken livers or they'll be as tough as old boots. The truffle is an optional luxury.

14oz fresh tajarin
salt and pepper
¼ cup butter
7oz chicken livers, chopped
1 teaspoon meat jelly (from the
  bottom of the jar of dripping),
  diluted in 2 tablespoons hot
  water

pinch of grated nutmeg
¼ cup grated Parmesan cheese
1 small truffle, preferably white
  (optional)
extra grated Parmesan cheese, to
  serve

In Italy, home-made pasta is usually made for special occasions or Sunday lunch. In many Italian families it is the young adolescent daughter who is given the job of rolling out the *sfoglia*, as it helps to develop a good bust!

Cook the *tajarin* in plenty of boiling salted water. Meanwhile, quickly melt half the butter over a fast flame until it foams, then throw in the chicken livers and stir them quickly to cook on all sides. Add the diluted meat jelly and nutmeg, and season with salt and pepper. Stir thoroughly, then remove from the heat.

Drain the pasta, transfer to a warm bowl, add the remaining butter and the cheese and mix carefully. Pour in the chicken livers and mix one more time. Shave the truffle all over the top of the dish, if used. Serve with extra cheese offered separately.

PAPPARDELLE CON I FEGATINI
Pappardelle with Chicken Livers

For this tasty dish from Venice, it is best to use fresh *pappardelle*. The unusual feature about the dish is that the *pappardelle* are not drained but must absorb all the broth as they cook. The actual amount of broth needed may vary, depending on the type of pasta, as some is more absorbent than others. I have given a guideline quantity of liquid but you may find you need more or less.

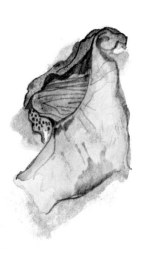

6 cups beef or chicken stock
2 tablespoons butter
8oz chicken livers, chopped
salt and pepper

14oz pappardelle (preferably
  fresh)
⅓ cup grated Parmesan cheese

Put the stock in a saucepan which is big enough to take all the other ingredients and bring to the boil.

Melt the butter in another saucepan and when it foams toss in the chicken livers. Turn them quickly to brown on all sides. Season with salt and pepper, then toss them into the boiling stock. Bring back to the boil, then add the *pappardelle*. When they are cooked, all the liquid should have been absorbed. Should this not be so, either drain some off or add if the pasta is not cooked.

Sprinkle with the cheese, stir carefully and turn out into a dish. Serve at once.

PAPPARDELLE ALL'ARETINA
Pappardelle with Aretina Sauce

In this recipe from Tuscany, it is best if you have the liver of the duck to finish off the sauce. If you don't have the liver, use 2 tablespoons of chopped chicken livers in the same way.

1 onion, peeled and chopped
1 carrot, scraped and chopped
1 stick celery, chopped
4oz prosciutto crudo (Parma, San Daniele or similar)
3 tablespoons butter

1 young duckling with its liver, quartered
salt and pepper
4 tablespoons tomato paste, diluted in 5 tablespoons hot water
14oz fresh pappardelle

In Lunigiana, a part of Italy which is now part of Tuscany, the earliest form of pasta was *testaroli*, which are pancakes of flour and water baked on a fire, then sliced and dressed just like pasta.

Fry the onion, carrot, celery and *prosciutto* in the butter until the onion is transparent. Add the duckling and brown on all sides. Season with salt and pepper. Add the diluted tomato paste and simmer very gently for about 1 hour or until the duck is cooked. Add a little hot water or stock if it should dry out.

Cook the *pappardelle* in plenty of boiling salted water, drain and transfer to a warm bowl. Pour over the sauce and mix together very thoroughly. Either place the duck quarters on top and serve the whole thing together, or serve the duck as a second course.

TORTIGLIONI ALL'ITALIANA
Tortiglioni Italian Style

One of the most traditional and perfect of all Italian dishes, this is very easy to make. But be sure you look after it carefully all the way through!

1 onion, peeled and chopped
3oz ham fat (from prosciutto crudo)
1/3 cup butter
4oz dried mushrooms, soaked for 20 minutes, rinsed and chopped
3oz lean prosciutto crudo (Parma, San Daniele or similar)
4oz chicken livers, chopped

5 tablespoons red wine
14oz canned tomatoes, drained and puréed
salt and pepper
14oz tortiglioni
6 leaves fresh basil, torn into pieces with your fingers
grated Parmesan cheese, to serve

Fry the onion with the ham fat and 1 tablespoon of the butter until the onion is transparent. Add the mushrooms and *prosciutto* and cook for 5 minutes, stirring constantly. Add the chicken livers, cook for a further 5 minutes, then add the wine and evaporate the fumes. Pour in the tomatoes, season with salt and pepper and stir. Leave to simmer, covered, for about 1 hour.

Cook the pasta in plenty of boiling salted water, drain and transfer to a warm bowl. Add the remaining butter and mix carefully, then add the sauce and mix again. Sprinkle the basil all over the top and serve. Accompany with freshly grated Parmesan offered in a separate bowl.

PASTA WITH MEAT

◆

Pasta evolved from being the staple diet of peasants and farmers to being everybody's daily fare. Those peasants and farmers would have kept a pig or pigs, which would have been made into ham, *salame*, sausages etc. and these preserved meats were then eaten together with pasta to make them stretch further. The first part of this chapter deals with preserved meats, but includes many highly sophisticated recipes which are a long way from being rustic peasant dishes.

The second part of the chapter is concerned with fresh meat. There are two basic ways to serve pasta with fresh meat: one is to braise or roast a piece of meat and use the juices for the preparation of the sauce; the meat itself is then served as a second course, after the pasta, with vegetables. The second method is to make a *ragù*, a sauce which originated in Bologna.

MACCHERONI ALLA CHITARRA
Guitar Maccheroni

Previous page: *Orecchiette al Sugo di Agnello*

This is the traditional dish of the Abruzzo area. If you want to make this kind of pasta yourself you need to have the special 'guitar' used to cut them on. This is a rectangle with fine steel wires stretched across it equidistantly. The sheets of dough (made of durum wheat, egg and water) are laid on top of the wires and then a rolling pin is rolled over the top to slice the pasta through the wires. Only in this way do you achieve the right shape. As a simple substitute, use the dry package variety or any thick fresh egg pasta, broken into short stubby pieces.

½ cup chopped bacon
14oz canned tomatoes, drained and puréed
salt and pepper

¼ cup butter
14oz maccheroni alla chitarra or similar
⅓ cup grated pecorino cheese

Fry the bacon until the fat is running, then add the tomatoes and season with salt and pepper. Simmer for 20 minutes, then add the butter and remove from the heat.

Cook the pasta, drain and transfer to a warm bowl. Pour over the sauce and the cheese, mix together and serve.

TAGLIATELLE CON PROSCIUTTO E PANNA
Tagliatelle with Ham and Cream

For this recipe you really do need good fresh *tagliatelle*. You can either make it yourself or buy it in one of the many shops and supermarkets that now supply it.

14oz fresh tagliatelle
salt and white pepper
1 cup light cream
3oz prosciutto crudo (Parma, San Daniele or similar),

finely chopped
1 egg yolk
⅓ cup grated Parmesan cheese
1 tablespoon butter

Cook the *tagliatelle* in plenty of boiling salted water. Meanwhile, whisk together the cream, ham, egg yolk and half the cheese and season with salt and white pepper. Whisk these ingredients into a smooth cream.

Drain the pasta, transfer to a warm bowl, add the butter and mix together. Pour over the cream sauce, mix together again very quickly and serve.

FUSILLI ALLA NAPOLETANA
Neapolitan Fusilli

Fusilli symbolise everything which is most Neapolitan, and this is the traditional sauce that goes with them. This dish comes out best if made in a large shallow terracotta pan.

1 large onion, peeled and
* chopped*
1 clove garlic, peeled and
* chopped*
1 carrot, scraped and chopped
1 stick celery, chopped
1 tablespoon olive oil
½ cup chopped bacon
½ cup dry white wine

14oz canned tomatoes, drained
* and puréed*
2 tablespoons tomato paste
salt and pepper
¼ cup grated pecorino cheese
14oz fusilli
5oz mozzarella cheese, cubed
1 teaspoon dried oregano

Real *fusilli* are an expensive and time-consuming type of pasta to make. Correctly, they are long and thin and made by wrapping a long piece of the *sfoglia* around a knitting needle like old-fashioned *maccheroni*, but no machine has yet been invented which can do this. The *fusilli* which are sold dried in packets or served in restaurants are short twisted shapes whose correct name is *eliche*.

In a wide, shallow pan (preferably flameproof terracotta) fry the onion, garlic, carrot and celery with the oil and bacon. Cook until the onion is transparent, then add the white wine. Allow the alcohol to evaporate, then add the tomatoes and tomato paste, mix together thoroughly, season with salt and pepper and simmer for 40 minutes. Add the *pecorino* and mix again.

Cook the *fusilli* in plenty of boiling salted water; drain and transfer to the large pan. Mix together carefully over a very low heat, then add the *mozzarella* and oregano, mix together one last time and serve.

MALTAGLIATI AL SALAME
Maltagliati with Salame Sauce

Salame is produced all over Italy in many different forms, from the tiny *salame felino* to the huge *finnocchiona*. No real *salame* is ever pink – it should always be dark reddish-brown, with clear white spots of fat – and each kind has its own distinctive flavor. For this recipe, try to use a *salame* of medium size and with quite a smooth texture.

5oz salame, coarsely chopped
3 tablespoons butter
3 tablespoons cooking oil
½ teaspoon chopped fresh
* rosemary*

4 tablespoons dry white wine
14oz maltagliati
salt and pepper
2 eggs, beaten
½ cup grated Parmesan cheese

Fry the *salame* gently with the butter, oil and rosemary, then add the wine and allow it to evaporate over a fast flame. Throw the *maltagliati* into a large pot of boiling salted water and allow them to cook.

Meanwhile, put the eggs and cheese into a large bowl, season with salt and pepper and whisk very thoroughly. Drain the pasta and pour it into the bowl. Pour the *salame* and its sauce over the top, mix together very thoroughly and serve hot.

SPAGHETTI ALLA CARBONARA
Spaghetti with Ham and Eggs

There are many different stories about the origin of this dish. The one I like best is this: at the end of World War II, there was in Trastevere in Rome an *osteria* which was very popular with the American G.I.s. They would swarm into the place demanding 'ham 'n' eggs', which the host would dutifully prepare for them. But they would never eat his *spaghetti* because they didn't like his sauces. So the ingenious man had the idea for this recipe, thus combining the nearest thing he could make to 'ham 'n' eggs' with his beloved *spaghetti*. The result was a terrific success and is still one of the favorite pasta dishes everywhere. This is my own recipe, though there are many variations.

14oz spaghetti
salt and pepper
4 eggs, beaten
½ cup grated Parmesan cheese
tiny pinch of grated nutmeg

4 tablespoons heavy or light
cream (optional)
7oz bacon (smoked or
unsmoked), chopped
3 tablespoons butter

Some people say that the origin of *Spaghetti alla Carbonara* lies in the fact that it was the dish prepared by the *carbonari*, the coalmen, and it was named after them.

Cook the *spaghetti* in boiling salted water. Meanwhile, whisk the eggs and cheese together with the nutmeg, cream (if used), salt, and plenty of freshly ground black pepper. Fry the bacon quickly with the butter and keep warm.

Drain the *spaghetti* and pour into a warm bowl. Add the egg mixture and mix together thoroughly and quickly so that the eggs are just cooked, then add the bacon, mix again and serve as soon as possible.

PAGLIA E FIENO
Hay and Straw

It is the combination of green and yellow pasta in this dish which gives it its name. You can use either *tagliatelle, tagliarini* or *linguine* and it should really be fresh. But if you are in a hurry, you can also use the dried kind.

7oz green tagliatelle
7oz yellow fettuccine
salt and pepper
4oz cooked ham, in one slice,
finely chopped

⅓ cup butter
½ cup light cream
⅓ cup grated Parmesan cheese

Cook the pasta in plenty of boiling salted water. Meanwhile, fry the ham gently in half the butter until the fat is transparent. Add the cream, season with salt and pepper and stir over a very gentle flame until the sauce is just thick.

Drain the *tagliatelle*, add the remaining butter and mix together. Add the ham sauce and mix again. Pour out on to a serving dish, sprinkle half the cheese over the top and serve. Offer the rest of the cheese separately.

Right: (from left to right) *Spaghetti alla Carbonara; Paglia e Fieno; Vermicelli allo Zafferano*

VERMICELLI ALLO ZAFFERANO
Vermicelli with Saffron Sauce

A very pretty, bright yellow dish, this is perfect for an Easter feast or sunny lunch. It is very easy and quite quick to make. It is best, if you can get hold of it, to use the powdered saffron available in sachets. Otherwise, soak four threads of saffron in a little hot water and use this liquid, strained carefully.

14oz vermicelli
salt
1 cup light cream
4oz cooked ham, chopped
¼ cup grated Parmesan cheese
1 sachet of saffron powder,
* dissolved in 2 tablespoons hot*
* water*

2 egg yolks
paprika
1 hard-boiled egg yolk, finely
* chopped*
1 tablespoon chopped fresh
* parsley*

In cases where the sauce is very rich it is best to use a type of pasta which does not gather up too much sauce with each mouthful, such as *spaghetti, bucatini* or *vermicelli.*

Cook the *vermicelli* in plenty of boiling salted water. Meanwhile, warm the cream, then add to it the ham, Parmesan cheese and saffron. Mix thoroughly and remove from the heat. Add the raw egg yolks and whisk them in energetically.

Drain the pasta, put into a warmed bowl and pour over the sauce. Mix together with a little paprika. Sprinkle the chopped hard-boiled egg yolk and parsley all over the top and serve.

PENNE CON PROSCIUTTO E PISELLI
Penne with Ham and Peas

This is a great favorite with our children, although those more daring and sophisticated in matters of gastronomy prefer it made with sausages. I find it comes out best made with smooth *penne* but the lined ones will do perfectly. *Crestoni* also work very well with this sauce. Try using sausages instead of ham sometimes (remember to cook longer for sausages).

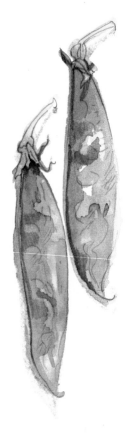

1 small onion, peeled and finely
* chopped*
2 tablespoons cooking oil
¼ cup butter
10oz shelled peas (fresh, frozen or
* canned), cooked*
6 tablespoons stock

5oz thickly cut cooked ham, cut
* into strips*
salt and pepper
14oz penne
2oz Gruyère cheese, cubed
¼ cup grated Parmesan cheese

Fry the onion gently in the oil and half the butter until transparent, then add the peas and cook gently, adding a little of the stock every now and again to prevent drying out. In a separate pan, fry the ham gently in the remaining butter, then add it to the peas. Season with salt and pepper and keep warm until required.

Cook the pasta in plenty of boiling salted water, drain and transfer to a warm bowl. Pour over the peas and ham, and mix together, adding the cheeses as you mix. Give it one last good stir to melt the cheese as much as possible and serve.

FETTUCCINE ALLA PAPALINA
Fettuccine with the Pope's Sauce

This dish was created in honor of a Pope several centuries ago. The name of the Pope has long since been forgotten, and so has the name of the cook who dreamed up this sublime concoction, but they say in Rome that nobody eats as well as the Pope!

1 small onion, peeled and chopped	3 tablespoons heavy cream
4oz prosciutto crudo (Parma, San Daniele or similar)	4 tablespoons grated Parmesan cheese
1/3 cup butter	14oz fresh fettuccine
3 eggs, thoroughly beaten	salt

Fry the onion and *prosciutto* with half the butter in a pan. Be sure to do this over a gentle heat so as not to toughen the ham. Beat the eggs, cream and half the cheese together in a bowl, then pour into a frying pan large enough to take all the pasta, once cooked.

Throw the pasta into a large pot of boiling salted water and when it is almost cooked, put the pan containing the cream and eggs on to a very low heat. Do not allow this mixture to scramble. Drain the *fettuccine* and add to the pan. Mix thoroughly with two forks, then add the ham mixture and the remaining butter. When it is all mixed very thoroughly, sprinkle the remaining cheese over the top and serve.

BUCATINI ALL'AMATRICIANA
Bucatini Amatriciana Style

This dish is the pride of Rome. I have had many arguments with people over the correct ingredients for it and everybody tells me something different! So at the risk of losing all my Roman friends here is a dish fit for Caesar himself. It is very important that the bacon should be crisp – the main characteristic of this dish is the contrast of the crunchy texture of the bacon with the hot spicy sauce.

Bucatini all'Amatriciana originate from Amatrice, a town in the Abruzzi near Rome, where they are famous for the rearing and butchering of pigs. The most important ingredient in this dish is a kind of bacon called *guanciale*.

6oz thickly sliced bacon, diced	14oz canned tomatoes, drained and chopped
2 tablespoons olive oil	
1 small onion, peeled and chopped	14oz bucatini
1/2 chili, chopped	salt
	1/3 cup grated pecorino cheese

Fry the cubes of bacon in the olive oil until the fat is transparent. Scoop out the bacon and put to one side to keep hot. Add the onion and chili to the remaining fat and fry until the onion is transparent. Add the tomatoes and cook for a further 20 minutes.

Cook the *bucatini* in boiling salted water. Meanwhile, add the bacon cubes to the sauce. Drain the pasta and transfer to a warm bowl. Pour over the sauce, add the cheese, mix together thoroughly and serve.

TRULLI AL SUGO DI OLIVE
Trulli with Olive Sauce

This is a delicious recipe and it is particularly nice to use *trulli*, that lovely pasta shape that is so rarely seen these days. If you can't find *trulli*, use any other short pasta.

1 onion, peeled and chopped	⅓ cup black olives, stoned and
4oz thick sliced bacon, chopped	cut into rings
into dice	⅓ cup green olives, stoned and
3 tablespoons olive oil	cut into rings
1 large yellow pepper (or red if	1 tablespoon capers, rinsed and
yellow is not available), cored,	squeezed free of vinegar
seeded and thinly sliced	1 teaspoon dried oregano
1lb canned tomatoes, puréed	salt and pepper
	14oz trulli

Fry the onion until transparent with the bacon and oil, then add the yellow pepper and fry for a further 10 minutes. Pour in the tomatoes and add the olives. Stir together and simmer for about 20 minutes longer. Finally, add the capers and oregano and season with salt and pepper. Stir again and leave to simmer gently until required.

Cook the pasta in plenty of boiling salted water, drain and transfer to a warm dish. Pour over the sauce, mix together very thoroughly and serve. No cheese is required.

LASAGNETTE PICCANTI
Lasagnette with Piquant Sauce

Some people may find this dish too highly flavored, but it is really delicious, and all the sharp flavors get the gastric juices working in readiness for the second course.

Lucania is probably the poorest area of Italy. The soil is not good enough to grow many crops and the parching sun beats down fiercely on what little will grow. Home-made pasta is, therefore, the solution to the problem of feeding their families for the housewives of these parts. There is very little meat or fish available, so their imagination runs riot with pasta, which is shaped into a hundred different forms and dressed with tomato and any available ingredients.

4oz smoked bacon, cut into strips	chili powder
1 large onion, peeled and sliced	2 heaped tablespoons capers
1 teaspoon chopped fresh sage	1 tablespoon wine vinegar
4 tablespoons cooking oil	large pinch of dried marjoram
10oz canned tomatoes, drained	14oz fresh lasagnette
and chopped	2 tablespoons butter
salt	¼ cup grated pecorino cheese

Fry the bacon, onion and sage in the oil until the onion is transparent, then add the tomatoes and simmer the sauce until thickened – about 20 minutes. Season with salt and a generous pinch of chili powder. Add the capers, vinegar and marjoram. Cook for a further 2 minutes, then remove from the heat.

Cook the pasta in plenty of boiling salted water, drain and transfer to a warm bowl. Add the butter, sauce and cheese, mix together thoroughly and serve.

Right: (top) *Farfalle con Sugo di Piselli;* (bottom) *Trulli al Sugo di Olive*

FARFALLE CON SUGO DI PISELLI
Farfalle with Peas

A very pretty and succulent dish, this is really easy to make. Use any other form of pasta you like, provided it is about the same size.

4oz smoked bacon, chopped
4oz unsmoked bacon, chopped
2 tablespoons cooking oil
1 tablespoon butter
8oz shelled peas (fresh, frozen or canned)

14oz canned tomatoes, drained and chopped
salt and pepper
generous pinch of dried oregano
14oz farfalle

Pasta with peas is traditionally served in Verona on the day of Saint Zeno, patron saint of the city.

Fry the two kinds of bacon with the oil and butter until crisp, then add the peas and tomatoes. Season with salt and pepper and simmer until the peas are cooked. Add the oregano and simmer for a further 5 minutes. Remove from the heat.

Cook the *farfalle* in plenty of boiling salted water, drain and pour into a warm bowl. Add the sauce, mix carefully and serve.

GRAMIGNA CON SALSICCIA
Gramigna with Sausage

Gramigna is a type of pasta used a lot in Emilia Romagna, which is where this dish comes from. It is like short stubby *spaghetti* and the easiest substitute is to break up *bucatini* into pieces about 2in long. If you cannot get hold of real Italian sausage, use the coarsest and strongest tasting sausage you can find.

14oz fresh sausages
28oz canned tomatoes, drained and puréed or tomato sauce (see page 12)

14oz gramigna or bucatini
salt
½ cup grated Parmesan cheese

Prick the sausages all over with a fork and put them in a frying pan. As soon as the juices are running, add the tomatoes or sauce and cook together gently for about 1 hour.

Cook the pasta in boiling salted water, drain and transfer to a warm bowl. Pour over the sausages and sauce and mix the whole thing together allowing the sausages to crumble at will. Add the cheese and mix again. Serve hot.

SPAGHETTI CON LE OLIVE VERDI
Spaghetti with Green Olives

An attractive looking dish, this is easy to prepare and delicious.

14oz spaghetti
salt and pepper
7oz smoked bacon, chopped
1 clove garlic, peeled and cut into
  thin slices
1 stick celery, chopped

1 tablespoon meat jelly (from the
  bottom of your dripping jar)
  diluted in 4 tablespoons hot
  water
1 tablespoon olive oil
⅓ cup grated Parmesan cheese
1 cup green olives, stoned, half
  chopped and the rest left whole

Cook the *spaghetti* in plenty of boiling salted water. Meanwhile, fry the bacon, garlic and celery together in a small pan for about 4 minutes. Add the diluted meat extract and cook for a further 5 minutes.

Drain the *spaghetti* and transfer to a warm bowl. Pour over the olive oil and mix together, then add the sauce and the cheese. Mix it all again, then add the olives and mix once more before serving.

PENNE ALL'ARRABBIATA
Angry Penne

These *penne* are called angry because they are very hot! You can increase the amount of chili if you like them even hotter and if you use Parmesan instead of *pecorino* you will find the dish has a more gentle flavor. True *Penne all'Arrabbiata* fanatics claim that to add onion is to ruin this dish! Please also note that you can remove the chili at any point during the preparation, though obviously the earlier you remove it the less the flavor and potency it will impart.

Chili is considered the best aphrodisiac in Italy, so to revive a flagging sex life or make a new baby (particularly if you want a boy), just make your man eat *Penne all'Arrabbiata* or *Spaghetti Ajo Ojo e Peperoncino* and he will "become a lion".

1 onion, peeled and very finely
  chopped
1 clove garlic, peeled and very
  finely chopped
1 red chili
4oz bacon fat, very finely sliced
  (about ¾ cup)
1 teaspoon butter

1lb canned tomatoes, drained
  and puréed in a food mill or
  processor or sieved
salt
14oz lined penne
½ cup grated pecorino cheese
1 teaspoon chopped fresh parsley

Put the onion, garlic, chili, bacon fat and butter into a pan and fry gently until the onion is transparent. Add the tomatoes and salt. Mix together very thoroughly, then cover with a lid and simmer for 20-30 minutes.

Cook the *penne* in plenty of boiling salted water, for about 7 minutes. Drain, transfer to a warm bowl and pour over the sauce. Remove the chili and mix together. Add half the cheese and mix again. Add a fine sprinkling of parsley over the surface. Serve with the rest of the cheese offered separately.

TAGLIATELLE ALLA BOLOGNESE
Tagliatelle with Real Bolognese Sauce

The Bolognese say that you cannot make a proper Bolognese sauce outside Bologna and, when I see what is served up under that name in some places, I have to agree! However, you can make a delicious, rich, meaty sauce that even a true Bolognese will be happy to eat. All it takes is love and care. *Il sugo*, as this Bolognese sauce is also called, becomes very personal to every cook who makes it. Italian cooks are nothing if not frugal and most housewives tend to pop any leftover bits of meat into their *sugo*; it works wonderfully and I urge you to follow their example.

I pity the poor cooks of Bologna! What extraordinary travesties does their famous pasta sauce take on once it crosses the frontier! Is it even recognizable as a Bolognese sauce by anything else other than its name on the menu? Here is the more elaborate and elegant version of the sauce, traditionally served with home-made pasta.

2½oz prosciutto crudo (Parma, San Daniele or similar), chopped
3 tablespoons cooking oil
1 small onion, peeled and chopped
1 small carrot, scraped and chopped
1 clove garlic, peeled and chopped
1 stick celery, chopped
10oz ground beef
1oz dried mushrooms, soaked for 20 minutes, drained and rinsed
5 tablespoons red wine

1 tablespoon chopped fresh parsley
½ tablespoon chopped fresh marjoram or ½ teaspoon dried marjoram
¼ teaspoon grated nutmeg
salt and pepper
½ tablespoon all-purpose flour
10oz canned tomatoes, drained and puréed
1 tablespoon tomato paste
14oz fresh tagliatelle
grated Parmesan cheese (optional)

Fry the *prosciutto* gently in the oil, then add the onion, carrot, garlic and celery. Fry until the onion is transparent. Add the beef and mushrooms, stir carefully and cook for 20 minutes. Add a little stock or water occasionally to prevent drying. Add the wine, herbs, and season with salt and pepper. Raise the heat to evaporate the wine. Stir for a few minutes, then add the flour. Mix in with care, then add the tomatoes and paste. Cook stirring for a further 10 minutes, then cover and leave to simmer very gently for about one hour.

While the sauce is simmering, make the *tagliatelle* (see page 155) or send somebody out to buy them – I do not advise leaving your sauce on its own for too long. Cook the *tagliatelle* in plenty of boiling salted water. Drain and pour into a warmed bowl. Pour over the sauce, mix together very thoroughly and serve.

Parmesan cheese can be mixed into the pasta with the sauce, and offered separately at the table.

LASAGNE AL SUGO
Lasagne with Sauce

This is a very unusual way of serving *lasagne*, because the sheets of pasta are layered but not baked. The dish looks very attractive if you cut the *lasagne* into squares and give them wavy edges by using a pastry wheel. The dish is from Liguria, where pasta cut like this is always called *lasagne*. Note the custom of burnt flour, which is typical of Genoese cuisine.

1 large onion, peeled and chopped
1 large carrot, scraped and chopped
1 stick celery, chopped
2 tablespoons chopped fresh parsley
⅓ cup butter
1lb very tender lean beef or veal, sliced into very thin strips

5 tablespoons white wine
14oz canned tomatoes, drained and puréed
salt and pepper
1 tablespoon all-purpose flour
1 cup stock
14oz fresh lasagne
⅓ cup grated Parmesan cheese

Fry the onion, carrot, celery and parsley in the butter until the onion is transparent. Add the meat, brown gently all over, then pour in the wine. Raise the heat to evaporate the alcohol fumes, then add the tomatoes. Season with salt and pepper, lower the heat and cover. Simmer for about 30 minutes.

Cook the flour in a separate pan until dark brown, then add it to the sauce. Stir thoroughly and leave to simmer for about 1 hour, adding a little stock every 10 minutes or so. Remove from the heat, and allow to rest while you cook the *lasagne*.

Cook the pasta in plenty of boiling salted water, drain and put one layer on a serving platter. Pour some sauce over this layer and cover with more pasta. Continue in this way until you have used up all the pasta. Pour the remaining sauce over the top, sprinkle over the cheese and serve at once.

In the city of Savona, in Liguria, the traditional Christmas dish is *maccheroni* with tripe.

GARGANELLI
Garganelli

Garganelli are a special form of pasta made in Emilia Romagna. This is the traditional sauce with which they are served. As the *garganelli* are rather complicated to make (see recipe page 157), I suggest you could also use this superb sauce to dress any form of home-made pasta.

1 carrot, scraped and chopped	*14oz canned tomatoes, drained*
1 onion, peeled and chopped	*and puréed*
1 stick celery, chopped	*salt and pepper*
¼ cup butter	*2oz chicken livers, finely chopped*
8oz ground beef or veal	*14oz fresh garganelli*
3 tablespoons white wine	*⅓ cup grated Parmesan cheese*

The *pettine* is the comb used to make *garganelli* in Emilia Romagna. The pasta dough is pressed across the teeth of the comb to make short, stubby *maccheroni.*

Put the carrot, onion, celery and half the butter into a saucepan and fry gently until the onion is transparent. Add the meat and brown it thoroughly. Add the wine and raise the heat to evaporate all the alcohol, then add the tomatoes. Season with salt and pepper, and leave to simmer over a low heat for 1 hour.

Add the chicken livers, cook for 4 minutes, and remove from the heat.

Cook the *garganelli* in plenty of boiling salted water, drain and transfer to a warm bowl. Add the rest of the butter, the sauce and the Parmesan, mix together very carefully and serve.

GASSE O PICAGGE AL SUGO
Gasse or Picagge with Meat Sauce

Gasse and *picagge* are two forms of pasta which are typical of the city of Genoa – turn to page 155 for how to make them. Either shape will do but you will have to make them yourself, so if you don't want to make the pasta, just use the sauce to dress any form of fresh pasta.

1 large onion, peeled and	*salt and pepper*
chopped	*1½oz dried mushrooms, soaked*
⅓ cup butter	*for 20 minutes, rinsed and*
10oz rump of veal, chopped very	*chopped*
coarsely or sliced	*1 tablespoon all-purpose flour*
14oz canned tomatoes, drained	*14oz gasse or picagge*
and chopped	*⅓ cup grated Parmesan cheese*

Fry the onion with the butter until transparent, then add the veal and brown it thoroughly. Pour in the tomatoes, season with salt and pepper and stir carefully. Bring back to simmering, then add the mushrooms. Stir, lower the heat and leave to simmer for about 30 minutes.

In a small pan, cook the flour until dark brown. Add it to the tomato sauce, mix thoroughly and cook for a further 20 minutes.

Cook the pasta in plenty of boiling salted water. Drain and transfer to a warm bowl. Pour over the sauce and the cheese, mix together and serve.

Right: (top) *Pipe con Gnocchetti di Carne;* (bottom) *Garganelli*

PIPE CON GNOCCHETTI DI CARNE
Pipe with Meat Dumplings

It takes about 3 hours to complete this dish, but if made well, it is worth every moment. The meat dumplings should be light and tender. The dish can serve as a main course, preceded by a light *antipasto*.

1 onion, peeled and chopped
3oz prosciutto crudo (Parma, San Daniele or similar)
3 tablespoons cooking oil
12-14oz braising beef, in one piece
6 tablespoons dry white wine
salt and pepper
1lb canned tomatoes, drained and puréed
1oz beef bone marrow

1 egg yolk
½ teaspoon grated lemon rind
1 ½ tablespoons dry breadcrumbs (brown or white)
1 clove garlic, peeled and crushed
1 tablespoon chopped fresh parsley
14oz pipe or other small, delicately shaped pasta
½ teaspoon dried oregano

In dishes where you want to eat more sauce than pasta, use shapes which will gather up a lot of sauce, such as *conchiglie*, *pipe* or *penne*.

Fry the onion gently with the *prosciutto*, then add the oil. Heat and add the meat. Brown the meat on all sides, then add the wine. Allow the alcohol to evaporate. Season with salt and pepper, then pour in the tomatoes. Stir and leave to simmer for at least 1 hour. If necessary, add a little hot water or stock during this time to prevent drying out.

When the meat is tender, remove it from the pot and mince it finely. Mix it with the bone marrow, egg yolk, lemon rind, breadcrumbs, garlic and parsley and season with salt and pepper. Be careful not to mix it too much. Shape into small balls with floured hands and put them into a shallow, wide pan. Only just cover them with cold water and simmer them very gently until cooked through (5-10 minutes from the moment the water boils).

Stir the sauce and check for seasoning. Cook the pasta in plenty of boiling salted water, drain and transfer to a serving dish. Add half the sauce and mix together. Lay the dumplings gently on top and cover with the remaining sauce. Sprinkle over the oregano and serve.

BOMBOLOTTI ALLA VALENTINA
Valentina's Bombolotti

This is a recipe of my own, which takes a very long time to cook. If possible I make it the day before I need to use it. An Italian housewife of the old school will get her pasta sauce, *il sugo*, going at seven o'clock in the morning in order to have it ready for lunch at one o'clock. I always serve the sauce with *bombolotti*, as rich meaty sauces sit best on big chunky pasta, but feel free to use it with any kind of pasta you like. Perfect for filling up hungry children.

1 onion, peeled and chopped
1 carrot, scraped and chopped
1 stick celery, chopped
2 cloves garlic, peeled and chopped
handful of as many fresh herbs as possible, chopped, or 1 teaspoon mixed dried herbs
½ cup butter
8oz ground beef, veal or rabbit (or any leftover meat, minced)

1 large marrow bone, sawn (by the butcher) into 2 or 3 pieces
2lb canned tomatoes, drained and puréed
2 tablespoons tomato paste
salt and pepper
14oz bombolotti, or other short chunky pasta
½ cup grated Parmesan cheese

Fry the onion, carrot, celery, garlic and herbs with half the butter in a large heavy saucepan. When the onion is transparent, add the meat and stir it around until lightly browned. Lay the marrow bone on top and pour in the tomatoes and paste. Stir, season with salt and pepper and cover. Put it on the minimum heat and let it simmer, very gently, for 3-4 hours. Stir occasionally.

After this time, remove from the heat and leave it to rest for as long as possible, preferably overnight. Heat through when required, stirring thoroughly, on a very low heat. Discard the marrow bone.

Cook the pasta in plenty of boiling salted water, drain and transfer to a warm bowl. Put half the remaining butter into the sauce and mix it around until it has vanished. Add the rest of the butter to the pasta. Mix together, then pour in three-quarters of the sauce and toss. Add half the cheese and mix again. Pour the remaining sauce on top, sprinkle the rest of the cheese over it and serve.

Note: Some people like to scoop the marrow out of the bones (if it's still in there after all that simmering!) and mix it up with the sauce and cheese.

In order to time his arrival and his lunch to perfection, it is quite common for the Italian working man to phone his wife just as he leaves the office with the sole command: *"Butta la pasta"* ("throw in the pasta").

ORECCHIETTE AL SUGO DI AGNELLO
Orecchiette with Lamb Sauce

The cooking of Puglia bears a strong Greek influence and, as in Greece, vegetables and lamb are used widely in their dishes.

If you make your own *orecchiette*, do remember they have to dry out for at least one whole day before you can boil them. The recipe is on page 157. However, the bought version are just as good and far less trouble. This dish is delicious, and also very simple, especially as the lamb itself can be served as a lovely second course with a fresh green salad. A recipe from Puglia.

2lb lamb (leg or shoulder)
3 tablespoons olive oil
½ cup butter

1 large sprig fresh rosemary or 1
*   teaspoon dried rosemary*
salt and pepper
14oz orecchiette
⅓ cup grated Parmesan cheese

Place the lamb in a flameproof casserole with the oil, half the butter and the rosemary. Season very thoroughly with salt and pepper. Put it over a low heat with a lid and, turning the meat every so often, allow it to cook very slowly. Add a small ladleful of water every now and again, to prevent the lamb from drying out, but also to produce the sauce. When the lamb is cooked, remove the fresh rosemary and the lamb from the casserole and set aside or serve as a second course.

Cook the *orecchiette* in plenty of boiling salted water. Drain and transfer to the casserole with the lamb's juices. Mix together very thoroughly with the rest of the butter and the Parmesan cheese. Turn out on to a platter and serve.

TAGLIATELLE 'SMALZADE'
Tagliatelle with Veal Stew

A stuffed pasta called *canederli*, sometimes filled with prunes, is the most typical savory dish in the Alto Adige region. The cooking of this region is much influenced by the fact that the Austrian border is only minutes away.

This dish really is a meal in itself, though if you want to make it a little lighter, omit the cream; although less rich and velvety, it will still be delicious. A recipe from far up North: Trentino-Alto Adige.

1lb shoulder of veal, cut into
*   cubes*
2 tablespoons all-purpose flour
⅓ cup butter
2 medium onions, peeled and cut
*   into quarters*

6 tablespoons dry white wine
½ cup stock
salt and pepper
14oz fresh white tagliatelle
5 tablespoons heavy or light
*   cream*

Toss the veal in the flour. Melt the butter in a large flameproof casserole and add the veal and onions. Brown the veal on all sides, then add the white wine. Allow the alcohol to evaporate a little, then add the stock and season with salt and pepper. Cover and leave to simmer for about 1½ hours, or until the veal is so tender it is almost falling to pieces.

Cook the *tagliatelle* in plenty of boiling salted water. Just before you drain the pasta, add the cream to the veal, stir through, then remove from the heat. Drain the pasta and transfer to a warm bowl. Pour over the sauce, mix together very thoroughly and serve.

ORECCHIETTE AL RAGU
Orecchiette with Meat Sauce

Another of my favorites. This is a dish from Puglia, the area where
orecchiette come from, in southern Italy. For this dish you must have
fresh basil, or the flavor will not be the same.

1 onion, peeled and chopped
1 stick celery, chopped
6 leaves fresh basil, torn into
  pieces with your fingers
5 tablespoons olive oil
10oz lean ground beef or veal

14oz canned tomatoes, drained
  and puréed
salt and pepper
14oz orecchiette
⅓ cup grated Parmesan cheese

Fry the onion, celery and basil in the olive oil until the onion is
transparent. Add the meat, brown it thoroughly, then add the
tomatoes. Season carefully with salt and pepper. Cover and simmer
for about 40 minutes.

 Cook the *orecchiette* in plenty of boiling salted water, drain and
transfer to a warm bowl. Pour over the sauce, mix, add three-quarters
of the cheese and mix again. Sprinkle the remaining cheese over the
top and serve.

ORECCHIETTE CON BRACIOLETTE
Orecchiette with Pork and Veal

This is a very filling and delicious dish, for which you need some
cacioricotta – baked, dry *ricotta* cheese. This could prove difficult to
find, so it can be left out altogether, or replaced by any strong-tasting,
salty, gratable cheese. Dried *chèvre* (goat's cheese) is one possibility.

4 slices of veal scallop
4 slices of fillet or boned loin of
  pork
8 slices of bacon
3oz Parmesan cheese
3oz pecorino cheese
2 tablespoons chopped fresh
  parsley
salt and pepper

1 large onion, peeled and
  chopped
3 tablespoons cooking oil
5 tablespoons red wine
12oz canned tomatoes, drained
  and puréed
14oz orecchiette
¼ cup grated cacioricotta cheese

The custom of serving pasta with
slices of meat is of Austrian origin
and is most common in the areas
closest to Austria. When pasta is
eaten in this way, the traditional
soup plate is abandoned and a
large flat oval platter is used by
each person.

Flatten the slices of meat with a meat mallet and lay a slice of bacon on
each slice. Place a small wedge each of Parmesan and *pecorino* cheese
on each slice, then add a little parsley and a small amount of freshly
ground black pepper. Roll up each slice of meat and tie it securely
with string. Grate the remaining Parmesan and *pecorino*.

 Fry the onion in the oil until transparent. Lay the meat rolls on top
and brown on all sides. Add the wine and allow the alcohol to
evaporate. Pour in the tomatoes and leave to simmer, covered, for
about 1½ hours.

 Cook the *orecchiette* in plenty of boiling salted water, drain and
transfer to a warm bowl. Pour over the sauce, mix together, add the
grated cheeses and mix again. Lay the meat rolls on the top and serve.

STUFFED PASTA

Every town in Italy seems to have its own traditional variety of stuffed pasta, but the idea behind them all is the same: the presentation of a delicious, succulent filling encased in a fine shell of the best fresh pasta and coated with butter and cheese, a good broth or sauce. In Italy, few housewives go to the trouble of making their own nowadays, unless it is for a special occasion. In every town you will now find a store which sells a variety of delicious, freshly-made stuffed pasta and many supermarkets also supply them. They are all quite good, but there is nothing to beat a plate of *tortellini* or *ravioli* which has been prepared at home with love and care.

Pasta which is to be stuffed must be made as fine as possible – some experts say you should be able to read a newspaper through it! It is the filling you are presenting, the pasta serves only as a shell and should therefore never be thick or heavy. Also, do make sure the edges of the pasta are securely sealed around the filling.

RAVIOLI ALLA MILANESE
Milanese Ravioli

Previous page: *Ravioli al Pomodoro*

These *ravioli* have quite a rich filling, so their accompanying sauce is simply the juices from a good roast. If you can't use the traditional sauce because you are not following the dish with a roast, then just use melted butter and cheese.

FOR THE FILLING
8oz cooked chicken meat, minced or processed in a food processor
1 lamb's brain
5oz beef bone marrow
1oz butter
1 heaped tablespoon grated Parmesan cheese
1oz fresh white bread crumbs
2 egg yolks
pinch of grated nutmeg
salt and pepper

FOR THE PASTA
3 ½ cups all-purpose flour
4 eggs
salt

TO SERVE
juices from a roasted joint
1 tablespoon butter
⅓ cup grated Parmesan cheese
OR
½ cup butter, melted and hot
½ cup grated Parmesan cheese

In Borgotaro, they make a type of *ravioli* which are called *malfatti*, meaning "badly-made", because they are rather fat and clumsy-looking. In contrast, they have a very delicate flavor.

Make the filling first. Place the minced chicken in a bowl. Blanch the brain in boiling water, drain and mince. Add it to the chicken. Soften the marrow in hot water, scoop it out and add to the chicken and brain. Mince the brain, chicken and marrow together (easily done in a food processor), then add the butter, cheese, breadcrumbs, egg yolks and nutmeg. Season with salt and pepper. Knead this mixture together with your hands. Make the pasta with the flour, eggs and salt, and fill and seal the *ravioli* (see page 156). Leave them to rest for 15 minutes.

Cook the *ravioli* in plenty of boiling salted water, drain and transfer half of them to a warmed bowl. Dress this half with the juices of the roast (or melted butter), then add the second half of the *ravioli* and more dressing. Toss carefully, add the cheese and toss again, then serve.

RAVIOLI ALLA GHIOTTA
Lipsmacking Ravioli

This is really the name of this dish, and once you've tasted it you'll know why! It would save you a lot of bother if you made the sauce the day before.

FOR THE FILLING
1 onion, peeled and chopped
5oz prosciutto crudo (Parma, San Daniele or similar)
1 tablespoon cooking oil
2 tablespoons butter
8oz ground veal
5 tablespoons dry white wine
4 tablespoons meat jelly (from the dripping jar)
pinch of grated nutmeg

salt and pepper
1 egg
FOR THE PASTA
3 ½ cups all-purpose flour
4 eggs
salt

TO SERVE
2 tablespoons butter
il sugo (see page 13)
⅓ cup grated Parmesan cheese

Make the sauce, *il sugo*, first, if you haven't already done so, so that it can simmer gently while you make everything else. If you have already made it, give it a good stir and put it back on the lowest possible heat to keep warm while you proceed.

Next, make the filling. Fry the onion gently with the ham, oil and butter until transparent. Add the veal and cook, turning constantly, until browned. Pour in the wine and raise the heat to evaporate the alcoholic fumes, then add some of the meat jelly and continue to cook until the veal is quite done. Add a little meat jelly every so often to give more flavor. Remove from the heat, add the nutmeg and season with salt and pepper. Let it cool, then add the egg and mix it in with your hands.

Make the pasta with the flour, eggs and salt and fill and seal the *ravioli* (see page 156). Let the *ravioli* rest under a dishcloth for 15 minutes. Cook the *ravioli* in plenty of boiling salted water, drain and transfer half of them to a warm bowl. Add the butter, half the sauce and half the cheese, and toss together carefully. Then add the remaining *ravioli* and cheese, mix together gently but thoroughly and serve.

CULIGIONES
Culigiones

Culigiones are Sardinian *ravioli* and for them to be really Sardinian you need to dress and fill them with Sardinian *pecorino* cheese. This is available in the better international delicatessens. The only possible substitute is very fresh *pecorino* for the filling and some seasoned *pecorino* for the dressing without worrying too much about whether they are Sardinian. If the flavor of the old *pecorino* is too much for you, use ordinary Parmesan.

It is thought that stuffed pasta was introduced to Italy in the 11th Century from Byzantium, along with the first primitive fork, when a sister of the Emperor Michael VII of Byzantium married a Venetian Doge. At the time the Byzantine cuisine was the most refined in the world.

FOR THE FILLING
8oz cooked spinach, very finely chopped
2 tablespoons butter
2 eggs
10oz softest pecorino Sardo cheese, very finely chopped
pinch of grated nutmeg
salt and pepper
1-2 tablespoons all-purpose flour

FOR THE PASTA
1 ¼ cups very finely ground semolina
3 eggs
salt

TO FINISH
tomato sauce (see page 12)
¼ cup grated pecorino cheese (seasoned)

Toss the spinach in a pan with the butter, then place it in a bowl and add the eggs, and nutmeg. Season with salt and pepper. Mix together with your hands. Bind it all together with the flour, and set it aside.

Make the pasta, using the semolina instead of ordinary flour, the eggs and salt (see page 154). Use the filling to make the *culigiones*, which should be the same shape but slightly larger than normal *ravioli*. Leave to rest for 15 minutes, then cook them in plenty of boiling salted water. Meanwhile, heat through the tomato sauce.

Drain the pasta, transfer to a warmed serving dish and pour over the sauce. Sprinkle the seasoned *pecorino* generously over the whole dish. Carry to the table with another bowl of grated *pecorino*.

ANOLINI ALLA PARMIGIANA
Anolini Parma Style

Parma is the home of the best ham and Parmesan cheese in Italy. Eating well is taken very seriously in that town, and it therefore goes without saying that this dish – their own type of stuffed pasta – is very special.

FOR THE SAUCE
1 onion, peeled and chopped
1 carrot, scraped and chopped
1 stick celery, chopped
2 cloves garlic, peeled and chopped
¼ cup butter
3 tablespoons oil
10oz beef sirloin or rump steak, in one piece
4 tablespoons dry red wine
14oz canned tomatoes, drained and puréed

salt and pepper
grated Parmesan cheese, to serve
FOR THE FILLING
6 tablespoons grated toast
1 egg
pinch of grated nutmeg
pinch of ground cinnamon
salt and pepper
FOR THE PASTA
2½ cups all-purpose flour
3 eggs
salt

Anolini are the traditional stuffed pasta of the city of Parma, where they are filled with braised beef and cooked in a traditional pot rather like a terracotta bowl.

For the sauce, put the onion, carrot, celery and garlic into a saucepan with the butter and oil and fry gently until the onion is transparent. Add the meat and brown it on all sides. Add the wine, raise the heat and let the alcohol evaporate. Then add the tomatoes and season with salt and pepper. Place a lid on top and leave this sauce to simmer for at least 2 hours, stirring occasionally. Add a little water if it appears too dry.

Put the grated toast in a bowl and dampen it with 4 tablespoons of the sauce. Bind with the egg, add the spices and season with salt and pepper. The filling should be of a very thick consistency.

Make the pasta with the flour, eggs and salt (see page 154). Roll out as finely as possible and cut into rounds with a glass or pastry cutter. Place a very small amount of filling in the center of each round, fold in half and press the edges together very firmly to seal perfectly – be sure they really are sealed or they will lose their filling when it comes to boiling them. (The characteristic of *anolini* is that they have no groove or pattern on the edges, unlike *ravioli*, *pansoti* and other stuffed pastas.) Leave them to rest for 15-20 minutes.

Cook the *anolini* in plenty of boiling salted water. Drain and transfer to a warmed platter. Pour over the sauce, keeping the meat aside for a second course, and toss gently. Sprinkle a generous handful of Parmesan over the top and serve, accompanied by a bowl full of freshly grated Parmesan.

RAVIOLI ALLA GENOVESE
Genoese Ravioli

This dish calls for the *ravioli* to be filled with Swiss chard, which can be replaced by spinach if you really cannot get hold of chard. The sauce is made with mushrooms and is delicious with any pasta. If fresh *funghi porcini* (*Boletus edulis*, ceps) are not available, dried may be used instead. Soak them, rinse, drain and dry before using. Borage is a lovely summer herb with a mild cucumber flavor. Replace with chopped herbs, spinach or more chard if unavailable.

FOR THE FILLING
7oz swiss chard, boiled and
  chopped
7oz fresh borage, boiled and
  chopped
7oz ground veal
1 tablespoon butter
4oz calf's brain, blanched and
  minced
4oz veal sweetbreads, blanched,
  skinned and minced
4 tablespoons fresh white
  breadcrumbs
3 tablespoons stock
¼ cup grated Parmesan cheese
salt and pepper
1 egg

FOR THE PASTA
3 ½ cups all-purpose flour
4 eggs
salt
FOR THE SAUCE
2 cloves garlic, peeled and
  crushed
½ cup butter
1 tablespoon chopped fresh
  parsley
12oz fresh funghi porcini,
  chopped
8oz canned tomatoes, drained
  and chopped
salt and pepper
⅓ cup grated Parmesan cheese,
  to serve

Make the filling first. Put the chard and borage in a large bowl. Fry the veal in the butter until well browned and add it to the vegetables. Mix thoroughly, then add the brain, sweetbreads, breadcrumbs, stock and cheese. Season with salt and pepper. Break in the egg and knead with your hands. You should have a paste which is not too sticky or wet. If you feel it is too sticky add another egg yolk or a little flour. Check the seasoning and set to one side.

Make the pasta with the flour, eggs and salt, and fill and seal the *ravioli* (see page 156); let them rest for 15 minutes. Meanwhile, fry the garlic gently in half the butter for 10 minutes, then add the parsley and mushrooms and continue to cook very gently. Add the tomatoes, season with salt and pepper and simmer until the mushrooms are completely soft. Set aside in a warm place.

Cook the *ravioli* in plenty of boiling salted water, drain and transfer half of them to a warmed bowl. Pour over half the sauce and mix together, then add the rest of the sauce, the remaining butter and the cheese. Mix together carefully and serve.

Sweet *ravioli* are a traditional speciality of the carnival period in Liguria. They are often served to children at teatime and you can smell them frying as you walk about the festive streets of Ligurian towns and villages in February.

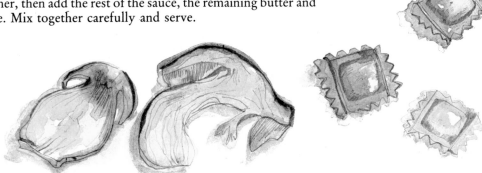

TORTELLINI ALLA BOLOGNESE
Bolognese Tortellini

In Tasso's story about the invention of *tortellini*, Venus was wandering, lost and alone, in the strange world of the Middle Ages. Seeking refuge in an inn for the night, she was spied on by the lecherous innkeeper. But the door was locked so he had to peer through the keyhole, and all he could see was her navel. He immediately rushed to his kitchen and created the *tortellino* as a eulogy to her superb belly button!

According to Tasso, it was a Bolognese inn that poor lost Venus was in when spied on by the innkeeper, so it is considered that Bologna is, among other wonders, the birthplace of the *tortellino*. Here is the great dish, presented in its most traditional and classic form.

FOR THE FILLING
2 tablespoons butter
4oz boned pork
3oz turkey breast meat
3oz boned veal
2oz lamb's brain, blanched
4oz mortadella
2 egg yolks
½ cup grated Parmesan cheese
grated nutmeg
salt and pepper

FOR THE PASTA
4 cups all-purpose flour
3 eggs
2 egg shells full of water
salt
1 teaspoon olive oil (optional)
TO SERVE
½ cup butter, melted or tomato
sauce (see page 12), il sugo (see
page 13) or ragù alla bolognese
(see page 14)
½ cup grated Parmesan cheese

Make the filling first. Melt the butter and add the pork, turkey and veal. Cook for about 10 minutes over a gentle heat, then add the brain and *mortadella*. Stir together over the heat for 5-10 minutes. Mince or process finely. Transfer to a bowl. Add the egg yolks and Parmesan, season with nutmeg, salt and pepper, and knead together with your hands. Put to one side.

Make the pasta with the flour, eggs, water, salt and oil, if used. Fill and seal the *tortellini* (see page 156). Let them rest for 20 minutes.

Cook the *tortellini* in plenty of boiling salted water, drain and transfer to a warmed platter. Pour over the melted butter (more if you wish), sprinkle over the cheese and serve. Alternatively, pour over the sauce of your choice, sprinkle over the cheese and serve after 5 minutes rest, to allow the sauce to seep into the pasta. Serves 6.

CAPPELLETTI ALLA PANNA
Cappelletti in a Cream Sauce

Quite often it is *tortellini* which are served with this traditional and elegant sauce, but in my opinion there is very little difference between them and *cappelletti*. Perhaps the *cappelletti* are a little smaller, but that varies so much – depending on who makes them. In any case, they are both wonderful!

The stuffed pasta most common in the Lombardy area is *agnolini*, which are a kind of *tortellini* with a double sheet of pasta covering the filling.

FOR THE FILLING
3 tablespoons butter
4oz ground pork
4oz ground veal
¼ cup grated Parmesan cheese
pinch of grated nutmeg
1 tablespoon fresh white
  breadcrumbs
4oz prosciutto crudo (Parma, San
  Daniele or similar), very finely
  chopped
salt and pepper
2 tablespoons hot stock

1 tablespoon chopped fresh
  parsley
FOR THE PASTA
3 ½ cups all-purpose flour
4 eggs
salt
FOR THE SAUCE
¼ cup butter, melted
3 leaves fresh sage
1 cup light cream
⅓ cup grated Parmesan cheese,
  to serve
white pepper

Put the butter in a saucepan and add the meats. Mix together until cooked through, then transfer to a bowl. Add the cheese, nutmeg, breadcrumbs and *prosciutto* and mix together evenly. Season with salt and pepper and add the stock and parsley. Mix again, then leave to one side.

Make the pasta with the flour, eggs and salt (see page 154). Roll it out in two equal sheets and make the *cappelletti*. Leave them to rest.

Meanwhile, in a small saucepan, heat the butter with the sage leaves for 5 minutes. Discard the sage and pour in the cream. Heat through, season with salt and pepper, and set aside in a warm place until required.

Throw the *cappelletti* into a pot full of boiling salted water. Drain as soon as they are tender and transfer to a warm bowl. Pour over the cream sauce and mix together carefully. Sprinkle over the cheese and white pepper and serve at once.

CAPPELLETTI ROMAGNOLI
Cappelletti in the Style of Romagna

In Emilia Romagna it is said that when making pasta you should never mix the eggs into the flour with a fork or any metal instrument. According to these cooks, and they are the world experts in making *pasta all'uovo*, only the hands should be used and the dough should not contain any salt. They also claim that only eggs with a really brown shell should be used.

This recipe calls for fresh watercress, but if it is left out the dish will still be delicious, even though you will have lost the traditional touch. These *cappelletti* are always dressed with a good, rich *ragù* of your choice.

FOR THE FILLING
*8oz turkey breast meat, cubed
 (¾ cup)
3oz ground pork
3 tablespoons butter
5 leaves fresh sage
1 large sprig fresh rosemary
2oz ricotta cheese
2oz fresh watercress
¼ cup grated Parmesan cheese
1 teaspoon grated lemon rind*

*salt and pepper
large pinch of grated nutmeg
2 eggs*
FOR THE PASTA
*3½ cups all-purpose flour
4 eggs
salt*
TO SERVE
*good sugo or ragù of your choice
 (see pages 13-14)
⅓ cup grated Parmesan cheese*

Cook the turkey and pork in a saucepan with the butter, sage and rosemary. When it is cooked through, process or mince with the *ricotta*, watercress, Parmesan and lemon rind. Season with salt, pepper and nutmeg, then bind with the eggs, using your hands.

Make the pasta with the flour, eggs and salt, and fill and seal the *cappelletti* (see page 156). Allow them to rest.

Cook the *cappelletti* in plenty of boiling salted water, drain and transfer to a warm platter. Dress with the *sugo* or *ragù*, toss together gently, sprinkle over the cheese and serve.

RAVIOLI CON IL RIPIENO DI PESCE E SPINACI
Ravioli with Fish and Spinach Filling

This is a really healthy dish as spinach and fish are both very good for you. Any white fish will do, though I prefer cod. Alternatively, you can use flaked fresh trout.

FOR THE FILLING
*1lb spinach, boiled and finely
 chopped
2 teaspoons anchovy paste
3 tablespoons olive oil
10-14oz white fish or trout fillets,
 chopped*

pepper
FOR THE PASTA
*3½ cups all-purpose flour
4 eggs
salt*
TO SERVE
⅓ cup butter, melted

Put the spinach, anchovy paste and olive oil in a pan and toss together gently to flavor the spinach. Then add the fish and a little freshly ground black pepper and heat, stirring, until the fish is cooked through. Push this mixture through a food mill, or process for 1 minute, to achieve a smooth paste.

Make the pasta with the eggs, flour and salt, and fill and seal the *ravioli* (see page 156). Let them rest for 15-20 minutes.

Cook the *ravioli* in plenty of boiling salted water, drain them and transfer to a warm bowl. Pour over the melted butter and serve.

Right: (from top)
*Cappelletti Romagnoli; Ravioli
alla Vegetariana; Ravioli di
Magro alla Panna*

RAVIOLI DI MAGRO ALLA PANNA
Lean Ravioli with Cream

Lean *ravioli* are those which are filled with the classic Italian combination of spinach and ricotta, and in this delicious recipe the plump, well-filled *ravioli* are quickly tossed in butter and cream. Here 3 eggs and the corresponding quantity of flour are suggested, because the pasta should be paper thin, but if you can't manage with so little make it with 4 eggs and 3½ cups of flour.

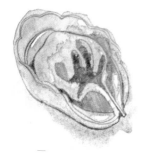

FOR THE FILLING
6oz spinach, boiled and finely
  chopped or puréed
¼ cup butter
salt and pepper
large pinch of grated nutmeg
6oz ricotta cheese, mashed to a
  cream
¼ cup grated Parmesan cheese

FOR THE PASTA
2½ cups all-purpose flour
3 eggs
salt

TO SERVE
¼ cup butter
1 cup light cream
¼ cup grated Parmesan cheese

Tortellini, ravioli or other stuffed pastas filled with ricotta and herbs are traditionally served in all parts of Italy, but particularly in Bologna, on Christmas Eve, when one should not eat meat.

Start with the filling. Heat the spinach in a large frying pan with the butter for 5 minutes. Add a generous amount of freshly ground black pepper, a little salt and the nutmeg and mix together very thoroughly. Add the mashed *ricotta* and Parmesan and work these ingredients together with a wooden spoon to a smooth consistency.

Make the pasta with the flour, eggs and salt, and fill and seal the *ravioli* (see page 156). Leave to rest for at least 30 minutes.

Cook the *ravioli* with great care in plenty of boiling salted water. Meanwhile, in a large pan, heat together the butter and cream but do not boil. Drain the *ravioli*, pour them into the cream mixture and toss them carefully and quickly while sprinkling the cheese over them. When you have covered them all thoroughly, turn out on to a platter and serve.

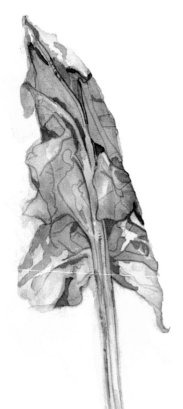

RAVIOLI ALLA VEGETARIANA
Vegetarian Ravioli

These *ravioli* are deep-fried, golden and crisp, then covered with a delicious tomato sauce. The dish is very popular with all our vegetarian friends.

FOR THE FILLING
2 eggplants, peeled and cubed
oil for deep-frying
20 walnuts, shelled and chopped
1 cup very thick béchamel sauce
  (see page 12)
1 tablespoon chopped fresh
  parsley
2 egg yolks

grated nutmeg
salt and pepper
FOR THE PASTA
3½ cups all-purpose flour
4 eggs
salt
TO SERVE
tomato sauce (see page 12)
⅓ cup grated Parmesan cheese

Deep-fry the eggplant cubes until golden, drain on paper towels and set aside. Reserve the oil. When the eggplant is cold, process it with the walnuts, béchamel sauce, parsley and egg yolks. Season with nutmeg, salt and pepper. If you haven't got a food processor just chop the walnuts very finely and mix the filling by kneading with your hands.

Make the pasta with the flour, eggs and salt and fill and seal the *ravioli* (see page 156). Let them rest for 10 minutes.

Deep-fry the *ravioli*, four at a time. Drain on paper towels. Arrange them on a warm platter, pour the tomato sauce over them and sprinkle on the cheese. Serve very hot.

RAVIOLI ALL'ABRUZZESE
Ravioli Abruzzi Style

These *ravioli* are not filled with meat but the sauce is very meaty. The filling is a sweetish *ricotta* mixture, which marries very well with the clovey flavor in the sauce. A real country speciality, made in the Abruzzi on special occasions.

There is a type of *ravioli* which is common both in the Venice and Trieste regions called *bauletti*. These were originally German and can still be found in Germany under the name *schlickkrapfen*.

FOR THE FILLING
12oz ricotta cheese
2 teaspoons sugar
½ teaspoon ground cinnamon
1 egg, beaten
FOR THE SAUCE
1 large onion, peeled and coarsely chopped
8oz ground beef, pork, veal or rabbit
⅓ cup butter
1 clove garlic, peeled and finely chopped
2 cloves
5 tablespoons dry red or white wine

10oz canned tomatoes, drained and chopped or sieved
salt and pepper
FOR THE PASTA
3 cups all-purpose flour
4 eggs
salt
1 egg yolk, beaten with 4 tablespoons cold water
TO SERVE
½ cup grated Parmesan cheese or ¼ cup grated pecorino cheese and ¼ cup grated Parmesan cheese, mixed together

To prepare the filling, mash the *ricotta* very thoroughly, or process to a smooth cream. Beat the sugar and cinnamon into the egg, then mix in the *ricotta* very thoroughly to form a soft filling. Set this aside while you make the sauce.

Fry the onion and the meat together with the butter until the onion is transparent, then add the garlic and cloves. Simmer gently for 10 minutes. Raise the heat and add the wine. Stir briskly while the wine evaporates, then pour in the tomatoes. Season with salt and pepper. Cover and leave to simmer for about 1 hour.

Meanwhile, make the pasta with the flour, whole eggs and salt (see page 156). Roll out the dough into two fine sheets of equal size. Brush one sheet with the egg yolk and water mixture and place the lumps of filling on top as normal. Lay the second sheet on top and cut and seal the *ravioli* as usual. Leave them to rest for about 30 minutes.

Cook the *ravioli* in plenty of boiling salted water. Scoop them out and place them on individual plates. Pour a ladleful of sauce over each portion, sprinkle with the cheese and serve at once.

AGNOLOTTI TRADIZIONALI
Traditional Agnolotti

Agnolotti originate from Piedmont, where they are filled with hundreds of different ingredients and dressed in many different ways. In many households in Piedmont it is customary to serve them on a Monday, thus using up the weekend's leftovers in the filling.

Agnolotti are plump pockets of fresh pasta which vary in shape from region to region.

FOR THE FILLING
*8oz boneless veal, pork and/or
  beef, sliced
2 tablespoons butter
3oz cooked spinach, chopped
2 slices of baked ham, chopped
3 slices salame (preferably
  Fabriano or Milano), chopped
1 teaspoon Marsala
4 tablespoons grated Parmesan
  cheese*

*grated nutmeg
salt and pepper*
FOR THE PASTA
*3 ½ cups all-purpose flour
4 eggs
salt*

TO SERVE
*juices from a roast, mixed with
  melted butter, or ½ cup butter,
  melted
½ cup grated Parmesan cheese*

Make the filling first. Fry the veal, pork or beef slices in the butter until cooked, then mince or process finely with the spinach, ham, *salame*, Marsala and cheese, season with nutmeg, salt and pepper.

Knead together the flour, eggs and salt for the pasta, and fill and seal the *agnolotti* (see page 157). Let them rest for a few minutes.

Cook the *agnolotti* in plenty of boiling salted water, drain and transfer to a warm platter or bowl. Pour over the melted butter with or without the juices of the meat you might roast as a second course, sprinkle over the cheese, toss carefully and serve.

RAVIOLI RIPIENI DI OSTRICHE
Ravioli Filled with Oysters

In his 'Don Juan', Cerere claims that in order to sustain a Don Juan-style love life it is vital to consume *vermicelli* with oysters and eggs.

This mouthwatering dish is best if made with a food processor; otherwise you need a pestle and mortar.

FOR THE FILLING
*2lb spinach, boiled and chopped
2 teaspoons anchovy paste
¼ cup pine nuts
2 cloves garlic, peeled and
  crushed
2 heaped tablespoons chopped
  fresh parsley*

*20 fresh oysters
2 tablespoons oil*
FOR THE PASTA
*3 ½ cups all-purpose flour
4 eggs
salt*
TO SERVE
tomato sauce (see page 12)

For the filling, process the spinach, anchovy paste, pine nuts, garlic and parsley for 1 minute. Alternatively, pound these ingredients thoroughly in a pestle and mortar. Open the oysters and pour their juices into the warmed tomato sauce. Add the oysters and oil to the filling and process or pound to a smooth paste.

Make the pasta with the flour, eggs and salt, and fill and seal the *ravioli* (see page 156). Leave to rest for 10-15 minutes.

Cook the *ravioli* in plenty of boiling salted water. Drain and arrange on a hot platter. Pour over the tomato sauce and serve.

Right: (top) *Tortelloni Verdi Gratinati;* (bottom) *Agnolotti Tradizionali*

TORTELLONI VERDI GRATINATI
Green Tortelloni Au Gratin

This is a real gastronomic treat, both to look at and to eat. The secret is that the *mozzarella* must be hiding carefully under the sauce, to appear as a surprise when you come to serving it. The dish is a little complicated perhaps, but well worth it.

FOR THE SAUCE
1 large onion, peeled and finely chopped
4 tablespoons olive oil
5oz ground beef or veal
14oz canned tomatoes, drained and puréed, or equivalent tomato sauce (see page 12)
salt and pepper
FOR THE GREEN PASTA
7oz cooked spinach, finely chopped
2½ cups all-purpose flour

2 eggs
salt
FOR THE FILLING
5oz ricotta cheese
⅓ cup grated Parmesan cheese
pinch of grated nutmeg
pinch of salt
1 egg
TO SERVE
⅓ cup butter, melted
⅓ cup grated Parmesan cheese
4oz fresh mozzarella cheese, very thinly sliced

Cansonsei are the speciality of Brescia and constitute the main dish at wedding receptions and other formal festivities. They are made in many different shapes with different fillings.

Make the sauce first so that it has time to simmer gently while you prepare the rest of the dish. Fry the onion in the olive oil until transparent, then add the ground beef or veal and brown gently without toughening. Pour in the tomatoes or tomato sauce, mix together very thoroughly, season with salt and pepper and cover with a lid. Leave to simmer gently, stirring every so often.

Process the spinach or push through a food mill, then make the green pasta with the flour, eggs, salt and spinach (see page 154).

For the filling, mash the *ricotta* with the Parmesan, nutmeg and salt, then bind it together with the egg, using your hands. Use this filling to make the *tortelloni*. Leave them to rest. Meanwhile, generously butter an ovenproof dish.

Cook the *tortelloni* in plenty of boiling salted water, drain and pour back into the saucepan. Pour over the melted butter and mix together. Add half the Parmesan and mix again, then transfer to the ovenproof dish. Arrange the *mozzarella* all over the top, then cover with the sauce. Sprinkle the last of the Parmesan over it and place under a preheated hot broiler. Cook for 5-6 minutes. Remove from the broiler and serve at once.

PANSOTI CON LE NOCI ALLA LIGURE
Pansoti with Nuts Ligurian Style

This is a very different recipe, in that the pasta is made with flour and wine, and the sauce is made from crushed walnuts and sour milk. Sour milk in Genoese is called *prescinseua* and is much used in Ligurian cooking, as are nuts and herbs, particularly basil.

FOR THE FILLING
1lb mixed fresh herbs (including plenty of fresh basil)
4oz fresh borage
1 egg
2 cloves garlic, peeled and crushed
4oz ricotta cheese
¼ cup grated Parmesan cheese
salt and pepper
FOR THE PASTA
3½ cups all-purpose flour

4 tablespoons dry white wine (or more as required)
salt
FOR THE SAUCE
1 cup shelled walnuts
4 tablespoons fresh white breadcrumbs, soaked in water and squeezed dry
4 tablespoons olive oil
4 tablespoons sour milk
salt
½ cup grated Parmesan cheese, to serve

Start by making the filling. Boil the mixed herbs and borage in very little water until wilted. Drain, squeeze dry and chop finely. Mix with the egg, garlic, *ricotta* and Parmesan and season with salt and pepper. Stir carefully for about 20 minutes to bind thoroughly or process for 1 minute. Set aside.

To make the pasta: pile the flour into its usual *fontana* and make a hole in the center. Pour in the wine, add salt and knead, gradually adding more wine as you need it to make a smooth but quite solid dough. Roll it out as normal a few times, then roll it out as finely as possible and cut into triangles with a pastry wheel. Each side of each triangle should be about 3in long. Place a small lump of filling in the center of each triangle, brush the edges with water, fold each triangle in half and press firmly to seal. Let the *pansoti* rest while you make the sauce.

Boil the shelled walnuts for a few minutes, then drain and peel carefully. Place the peeled walnuts in a mortar and pound thoroughly, or process for 45 seconds, with the breadcrumbs. When you have reduced this mixture to a soft purée, turn it into a bowl. Add the oil and sour milk alternately, stirring constantly. Add a little salt and stir until really velvet smooth, then set aside.

Cook the *pansoti* in plenty of boiling salted water, drain and transfer to a platter. Pour over the sauce, sprinkle half the cheese over the dish and serve with the rest of the cheese offered separately.

Pansoti, the Ligurian stuffed pasta, means "fatties", that is rounded tummies. If you look carefully at a nice plump *pansoto*, it is easy to see why!

RAVIOLI CON LA ZUCCA
Ravioli with Pumpkin

In this recipe, there are two very original ingredients that are not often used. They are the *mostarda di frutta*, which is a sweet but very hot pickle or form of candied fruit, and the *amaretti* which are very small Italian macaroons. I think that chutney (provided it is quite peppery) works quite well in the place of the *mostarda di frutta*, and the *amaretti* can be replaced by ratafia or macaroons. The dish is superb and very unusual – seldom found in an Italian restaurant.

FOR THE FILLING
4lb yellow pumpkin, baked in the oven in its skin, like a potato
½ cup grated Parmesan cheese
5 amaretti, crushed
7oz mostarda di frutta, finely chopped
large pinch of grated nutmeg
large pinch of ground ginger
salt and pepper

FOR THE PASTA
3 ½ cups all-purpose flour
4 eggs
salt

TO SERVE
½ cup butter, melted
5 leaves fresh sage
½ cup grated Parmesan cheese

Pumpkin-filled *ravioli* or *tortelli* are traditional dishes served on Christmas Eve in the Mantua region, followed by a large marinated eel and a stick of nougat *(torrone)*.

To make the filling, discard the seeds from the baked pumpkin, then scoop out the soft flesh and place it in a bowl. Add the Parmesan and mix it in, then add the *amaretti* and *mostarda*. Season carefully with the spices, salt and pepper and put to one side.

Make the pasta with the flour, eggs and salt and fill and seal the *ravioli* (see page 156). Allow them to rest for 15 minutes.

Cook the *ravioli* in plenty of boiling salted water. Meanwhile, in a small saucepan, heat the butter until hazelnut brown and place the sage in it. Keep warm.

Drain the *ravioli* carefully and arrange half of them on a warm platter. Pour over half the butter (remove the sage) and sprinkle over half the cheese. Arrange the rest of the *ravioli* on top. Pour over the remaining butter and sprinkle the rest of the cheese over that, then serve.

RAVIOLI RIPIENI DI RAGU DI PESCE
Ravioli Filled With Fish

Any delicate white fish will work very well for this fish and tomato filling. The *ravioli* can then either be coated with hot melted butter and Parmesan cheese, or you can save a little sauce and use that to dress them.

FOR THE FILLING
3 tablespoons olive oil
4 canned anchovy fillets, drained,
 soaked in milk and rinsed
1 onion, peeled and finely
 chopped
2 sticks celery, chopped
1 carrot, scraped and finely
 chopped
2 cloves garlic, peeled and
 chopped
3 tablespoons chopped fresh
 parsley
1oz dried mushrooms, soaked in
 warm water for 20 minutes,

rinsed and chopped
4 tablespoons tomato paste
 diluted in 3 tablespoons hot
 water
12oz white fish, skinned, filleted
 and chopped
salt and pepper
FOR THE PASTA
3½ cups all-purpose flour
4 eggs
salt
TO SERVE
⅓ cup butter, melted
¼ cup grated Parmesan cheese

Heat the olive oil in a saucepan with the anchovy fillets. Mash the anchovies to a smooth pulp, then add the onion, celery, carrot, garlic and parsley. Mix together very thoroughly and fry gently for 5 minutes. Add the mushrooms and cook for a further 5 minutes. Pour in the diluted tomato paste and mix together to form a thick sauce. Add the fish, stir together for a few minutes, season with salt and pepper and remove from the heat. Cool.

Make the pasta with the flour, eggs and salt, and fill and seal the *ravioli* (see page 156). If you want the filling to double as a sauce, keep some in the pan and add 2 tablespoons more tomato paste diluted in 6 tablespoons water. Warm through and keep aside.

Cook the *ravioli* in plenty of boiling salted water, drain and transfer to a warm bowl. Pour over the hot melted butter and the sauce if used and toss together with care. Sprinkle over the cheese and serve.

In Genoa it is still customary to eat *ravioli* filled with fish on a Friday, even though it is no longer a day when you cannot eat meat.

AGNOLOTTI TOSCANI
Agnolotti Tuscan Style

The best way to enjoy these *agnolotti* is to cook them in some really good stock and to eat the dish as a soup. If you don't like this way of having pasta, the usual dressing of hot melted butter and Parmesan cheese freshly grated over the top also makes for a superb starter.

FOR THE FILLING
1 cup fresh white breadcrumbs
5 tablespoons warm milk
5oz lean, boneless veal
3 tablespoons butter
8oz veal brain, blanched and
  chopped
1 egg
5 tablespoons grated Parmesan
  cheese

salt and pepper
FOR THE PASTA
2 ½ cups all-purpose flour
4 eggs
salt

TO SERVE
6 cups (or more if you like) good
  meat or chicken stock, or ⅓ cup
  butter, melted
⅓ cup grated Parmesan cheese

Agnolotti are always eaten on Christmas Day in Piedmont and in many villages they are also a traditional carnival dish.

Start by making the filling. Soak the breadcrumbs in the milk until soft. Fry the veal gently in the butter until cooked through, then mince it. Process or mince the breadcrumbs, brain and veal together, then add the egg and parmesan and season with salt and pepper. Knead with your fingers to a smooth paste.

Make the pasta with the flour, eggs and salt and fill and seal the *agnolotti* (see page 157). Allow them to rest for 20 minutes.

Cook the *agnolotti* in the stock and serve very hot as a soup, with the Parmesan offered separately; or cook in boiling salted water, drain and transfer to a warm platter. Pour over the melted butter, sprinkle on the cheese, toss once and serve.

CAPPELLETTI AL PISTACCHIO
Cappelletti with Pistachio Nuts

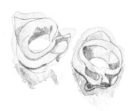

This recipe has nuts both inside and outside the *cappelletti*, making for a very distinctive crunchy texture as well as a superb flavor. If you draw the line at using brain it can be replaced by plain cooked ground veal, though the taste will not be the same.

FOR THE FILLING
8oz prosciutto crudo (Parma, San
  Daniele or similar), very finely
  chopped
5oz beef bone marrow, finely
  chopped
1 lamb's brain, blanched and
  chopped
½ cup grated Parmesan cheese
2 tablespoons butter, melted
pinch of grated nutmeg
salt and pepper
1 egg yolk

1 egg
¼ cup pistachio nuts, very finely
  chopped
FOR THE PASTA
3 ½ cups all-purpose flour
4 eggs
salt
FOR THE SAUCE
½ cup butter
½ cup pistachio nuts, finely
  chopped
½ cup grated Parmesan cheese,
  to serve

Mix together the *prosciutto*, marrow and brain. Add the Parmesan, butter and nutmeg, season with salt and pepper and mix again. Add the egg yolk and whole egg and the pistachio nuts. Mix very thoroughly (process for 1 minute if possible) and set to one side.

Make the pasta with the flour, eggs and salt, and fill and seal the *cappelletti* (see page 156). Let them rest for 15 minutes.

Cook the *cappelletti* in a large pot of boiling salted water. Meanwhile, melt the butter with the pistachio nuts in a small saucepan until nut brown. Keep warm. Drain the pasta and transfer to a warmed, wide platter. Pour over the butter with the nuts, sprinkle the cheese over them and serve without further ado.

RAVIOLI CON I FILETTI DI SOGLIOLA
Ravioli with Sole

In this recipe, the ravioli are filled with *ricotta*, Parmesan and seasoning and they are dressed with a delicious sauce of fillets of sole. A traditional speciality from the Marche region.

In Cremona, they make a kind of *ravioli* called *marubini*.

FOR THE PASTA
3 ½ cups all-purpose flour
4 eggs
salt
FOR THE FILLING
8oz ricotta cheese
4 tablespoons grated Parmesan
  cheese
pinch of grated nutmeg
salt and pepper
1 egg
FOR THE SAUCE
1 carrot, scraped and chopped

1 large stick celery, chopped
3 cloves garlic, peeled and
  crushed
5 tablespoons olive oil
2 soles (each weighing about
  8oz), cleaned and filleted
6 tablespoons dry white wine
14oz canned tomatoes, drained
  and puréed
salt and pepper
2 tablespoons chopped fresh
  parsley, to garnish

Make the pasta with the flour, eggs and salt (see page 154). Roll it out in two equal sheets.

Mash together the *ricotta* and Parmesan and season with nutmeg, salt and pepper. Bind it all with the egg, using your fingers. Use this filling to make the *ravioli*. Leave them aside to rest while you make the sauce.

Fry the carrot, celery and garlic together in the oil until soft. Gently lay the sole fillets on top and cook on one side, then turn carefully to cook the other side. Turn up the heat and add the white wine. Allow the fumes to evaporate, then pour in the tomatoes. Season with salt and pepper and lower the heat. Leave to simmer for about 15 minutes. Be careful not to overcook as the sole will fall apart, and it is important to keep it intact.

Cook the *ravioli* in plenty of boiling salted water, drain and transfer to a platter. Pour over the sauce, arranging the sole on top, sprinkle with the parsley and serve.

BAKED PASTA

Baked pasta seems to be popular with almost everyone and is my favorite standby for all occasions. For
informal dinners with friends, where the company
and conversation are as important as the food and
you are not going all out to impress anyone, these
simple dishes provide a perfect solution. You can
make everything in advance, all you need to
remember is to pop the dish into the oven in time.
Served with a salad, followed by a simple dessert and
there you have it: a superb meal created with a
minimum of fuss.

All these dishes (with the exception of *Maccheroni al Forno*) can be easily frozen and to do so I
suggest you follow the method I have used for years.
Instead of buttering the ovenproof dish, line it with
freezer clingfilm, then make the dish as usual. Fill
the dish to two inches from the top to allow for
expansion, wrap the clingfilm over the top and
freeze. When frozen, remove the parcel of pasta
from the dish and store as normal. When you want
to use it, dip the parcel into a basin of very hot water,
peel off the clingfilm and return the pasta to its
original dish, this time buttered. Thaw and bake as
usual, or place frozen in a cool oven until heated
through, then raise the heat to brown the top.

MACCHERONI E RICOTTA AL FORNO
Maccheroni and Ricotta Bake

Previous page: *Maccheroni e Ricotta al Forno*

It is quite a laborious process to prepare this properly, though you can take a short cut and use a prepared *ragù* or *sugo* (see pages 13-14).

1lb braising steak	*salt and pepper*
1 onion, peeled and sliced	*10oz canned tomatoes, drained*
1 carrot, scraped and chopped	*and puréed*
1 large stick celery, chopped	*1lb ricotta cheese, mashed*
1 clove garlic, peeled and	*½ cup grated Parmesan cheese*
chopped	*14oz maccheroni*
4 tablespoons oil	*2oz mozzarella cheese, diced*
5 tablespoons dry red wine	

Put the meat, vegetables and oil into a flameproof casserole and brown the steak thoroughly all over. Simmer for about 30 minutes, adding a little red wine every so often. Season with salt and pepper, then add the tomatoes. Simmer for a further 30 minutes, stirring occasionally.

Remove the meat and mince or process it finely. Mash the *ricotta* and add the minced meat and sauce. Mix it all together very thoroughly. Add half the Parmesan and mix again.

Cook the *maccheroni* in plenty of boiling salted water, drain and transfer to a bowl. Pour over the sauce and mix together very carefully. Transfer to a buttered ovenproof dish and sprinkle the remaining Parmesan and the *mozzarella* on the top.

Bake in a preheated 400° oven for 20 minutes, or until the top is bubbling and browned. Remove from the oven, rest for 5 minutes and then serve.

PASTA AL FORNO IN BIANCO
Baked Pasta in a White Sauce

Any short pasta will work very well for this family favorite. An easily digested and simple dish, it is quick and uncomplicated. Keep a few in the freezer.

14oz short pasta (penne, ditali,	*1 cup grated cheese: Parmesan,*
maccheroni, etc.)	*Cheddar, Bel Paese etc.*
salt and pepper	*7oz best baked ham, chopped*
2 cups béchamel sauce (see page	*¼ cup butter*
12)	

Cook the pasta in plenty of boiling salted water. Meanwhile, heat through the béchamel and melt the grated cheese into it. Drain the pasta and pour it back into the pot. Pour in three-quarters of the sauce and mix it together very thoroughly. Add the ham and mix again.

Grease a large ovenproof dish with half the butter, pour in the pasta and arrange it carefully. Pour over the remaining sauce and dot the remaining butter on top.

Bake in a preheated 400° oven for 20 minutes until bubbling and golden. Remove, rest for 5 minutes and then serve.

Matilde Serao wrote an absolutely delightful story about the invention of *maccheroni*. In the year 1220, there lived in Naples a magician called Chico. This Chico lived in a house where there also lived many other people of disconcerting habits: there was a prostitute on the second floor, a paid killer on the first floor and a group of expert thieves on the third floor. Chico lived in two rooms on the top floor and he never opened his shutters to the sun, nor did he ever come out. He would spend his days inventing something very mysterious and the gossips said they had seen him doing strange things in front of a huge pot of boiling water. Others claimed they had seen strange instruments in his hands and that he wandered about dressed in white. Every day Chico would send his faithful servant to the market to buy herbs and vegetables for him.

Next door to Chico lived Jovanella, the youngest cook at the royal court, and the greatest gossip in Naples. She tried for years to discover what Chico was doing until finally, one day, through the crack of a door, she saw what he was up to. He was making pasta, and the vegetables and herbs went into a sauce to pour over it! Jovanella raced off to the palace and begged to be allowed to cook the king her secret new dish. Of course, the dish was a huge success and before long Jovanella became an extremely popular and rich young woman.

MACCHERONI AL FORNO
Baked Maccheroni

This is just one of the recipes which bear the generic name *Maccheroni al Forno*. In this variation, fresh sardines are used. If they are not available, pilchards or infant herrings may be substituted. Use the smallest *maccheroni* available.

The word *maccherone* has been in use since 1041, when it was used to describe somebody who was a bit silly, a naive sort of chap.

14oz maccheroncini
salt and pepper
½ cup olive oil (use more if
 required)
10oz fresh sardines, cleaned and
 filleted
10oz canned tomatoes, drained
 and chopped

6 canned anchovy fillets, drained
1 tablespoon capers
4 tablespoons chopped stoned
 black olives
4 tablespoons fine dry
 breadcrumbs

Cook the pasta in plenty of boiling salted water, drain and transfer to a bowl. Pour over enough olive oil to dress the pasta lightly. Set aside.

Cook the sardine fillets in olive oil and set them aside too. Cook the tomatoes in a little olive oil over a fast flame until they are just falling apart, season with salt and pepper and set aside.

Grease an ovenproof dish with the rest of the olive oil. Arrange half the pasta on the bottom and spread the sardines, tomatoes, anchovies, capers and olives all over it. Cover with the remaining pasta and press it down with care. Cover completely with the breadcrumbs and drip a little olive oil over the top.

Bake in a preheated 300° oven for 20-30 minutes or until there is a crisp crust on the top, rest for 5 minutes, then serve.

CANNELLONI RIPIENI DI TONNO
Cannelloni with Tuna Fish Stuffing

This is a very easy dish and also economical. You can add other ingredients to the tuna fish to vary the dish – try peas, mushrooms, tomatoes or olives.

14oz lasagne (preferably white)
salt and pepper
2 cups béchamel sauce (see page 12)
13oz canned tuna fish (use less if adding other ingredients to the base), drained and flaked

3 tablespoons canned corn, drained
5 tablespoons grated Parmesan cheese
2 tablespoons butter

Cook the *lasagne* four at a time in plenty of boiling salted water, then lay them out on a wet cloth side by side to drain.

Heat through the béchamel sauce and pour half of it into a bowl. Add the tuna, the corn and half the cheese and season with salt and pepper. Mix together to a smooth paste. Fill each sheet of *lasagne* with this and roll them up into cylinders. Place them, sealed edge down, in a buttered ovenproof dish. Cover with the rest of the béchamel sauce. Sprinkle over the remaining cheese and dot the butter over them.

Bake in a preheated 400° oven for 20 minutes or until the top is golden brown and the dish is bubbling. Remove from the oven, rest for 5 minutes and then serve.

PASTA D'AVANZO AL FORNO
Leftover Baked Pasta

In the letters that Rossini wrote home while in Paris, he complains bitterly about the quality of the pasta available abroad. He signed himself "Rossini Senzamaccheroni" (without *maccheroni*) and asked for pasta to be sent to him from Italy.

Pasta often tastes better when reheated and leftover pasta drenched with a creamy sauce and baked in a hot oven until the top is browned and crisp is a truly celestial gastronomic experience! You can use almost any kind of pasta to create this dish: stuffed, fresh egg or plain. However, fish pasta does not normally work very well, nor do those pastas strongly flavored with garlic.

2 cups béchamel sauce (see page 12)
7oz cheese (mozzarella, Gruyère, Emmenthal, Gouda or Swiss), chopped

4 tablespoons grated Parmesan cheese
about 14oz leftover dressed pasta, preferably in a meat, tomato or mushroom sauce
½ cup butter

Butter an ovenproof dish big enough to take all the pasta and the sauce. Make the bechamel sauce and add half the cheese to it, including half the Parmesan. Melt the cheeses into the sauce thoroughly, then mix the sauce with the pasta and half the butter in a bowl. Turn it into the buttered dish, distributing the remaining cheese among it. Dot the rest of the butter on top and sprinkle on the remaining Parmesan. Place in the center of a preheated 400° oven and bake for 20 minutes or until the top is well browned. Rest for 5 minutes then serve from the dish.

Right: (left) *Lasagne con i Spinaci;* (right) *Cannelloni Ripieni di Tonno*

LASAGNE CON I SPINACI
Lasagne with Spinach

I sometimes make this dish with fresh green *lasagne*, but many people think it is altogether *too* green for a pasta dish. I have finally conceded that green and white is a better color combination, and allows for more color scope throughout the rest of the meal.

14oz fresh lasagne
salt and pepper
½ cup chopped unsmoked bacon
1 onion, peeled and chopped
4 tablespoons olive oil
8oz ground veal
2oz chicken livers, finely chopped
2oz dried mushrooms, soaked for
*   20 minutes, rinsed, drained and*
*   finely chopped*

2 tablespoons tomato paste,
*   diluted in 2 tablespoons boiling*
*   water*
1½lb cooked spinach, finely
*   chopped*
8oz ricotta cheese
2 tablespoons heavy cream
½ cup grated Parmesan cheese
1 egg
grated nutmeg

Cook the *lasagne* four at a time in boiling salted water, then lay them carefully on a wet cloth, side by side, to drain.

Fry the bacon and onion in the olive oil until the onion is transparent. Add the ground veal and brown carefully, then add the chicken livers and mushrooms. Mix together very thoroughly. Pour in the diluted tomato paste, season with salt and pepper and cover. Leave to simmer for about 40 minutes, stirring occasionally. Add a little boiling water if it appears to be drying out.

Mash the spinach with the *ricotta*. Add the cream, half the Parmesan and the egg and season with nutmeg, salt and pepper. Beat thoroughly with a wooden spoon (or process for 1 minute) until smooth and velvety.

Generously butter an ovenproof dish. Make a layer of *lasagne* on the bottom and cover with a layer of one sauce. Add another layer of *lasagne* and spread on a layer of the other sauce. Continue alternating the two sauces and pasta layers until you have used them all up. End with the meat sauce. Sprinkle the rest of the Parmesan over and dot the rest of the butter on top. Bake in a preheated 400° oven for about 20 minutes or until bubbling and golden brown. Rest for about 5 minutes before you serve it.

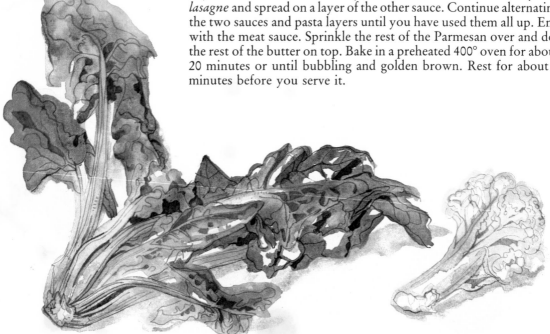

LASAGNE VERDI AL FORNO
Baked Green Lasagne

A very rich version of *lasagne*, this is a perfect supper party dish, as you can prepare it all in advance and pop it in the oven for 20 minutes once your guests arrive.

14oz fresh green lasagne
salt and pepper
1 onion, peeled and chopped
1 carrot, scraped and chopped
1 stick celery, chopped
1 clove garlic, peeled and
  chopped
4 tablespoons olive oil
4oz lean ground meat (veal
  and/or beef)

½ cup chopped cooked ham or
  bacon
4 tablespoons tomato paste
  diluted in 4 tablespoons boiling
  water
2 cups béchamel sauce (see page
  12)
½ cup grated Parmesan cheese
pinch of grated nutmeg
⅓ cup butter

Cook the *lasagne* four at a time in plenty of boiling salted water and then lay them gently side by side on a wet cloth to drain so they do not stick together.

Fry the onion, carrot, celery and garlic in the olive oil until the onion is transparent. Add the ground meat and brown gently for about 10 minutes. Add the ham or bacon and simmer again. Finally add the tomato paste and allow it all to cook gently for about 30 minutes. Season with salt and pepper and remove from the heat.

Warm the béchamel through with half the grated cheese and the nutmeg. Check the seasoning.

Butter an ovenproof dish and cover the bottom with *lasagne*. Spread a few spoonfuls of each sauce on it and then cover with more *lasagne*. Sprinkle Parmesan and dot butter between each layer as you go. Continue to fill the dish in this way until you have used up all the ingredients, finishing with béchamel. Dot the last of the butter on top and sprinkle on a little Parmesan.

Bake in a preheated 425° oven for 20 minutes, or until the top is well browned and crispy. Remove from the oven and allow to rest for about 5 minutes before serving.

There is a dish still served in Trieste, of *lasagne* with poppy seeds, which was particularly fashionable at the beginning of this century and which in German is called *mohnnudeln*. It has a sweetish flavour typical of the cooking in these parts and reflects the heavy Austro-Hungarian and Balkan influence which is felt to this day in the region.

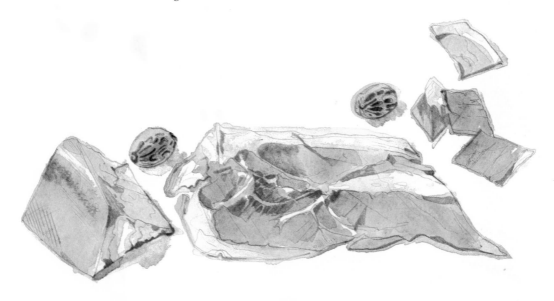

LASAGNE AL POMODORO AL FORNO
Baked Lasagne with Tomato Sauce

A delicious all-vegetable lasagne dish.

14oz lasagne
salt and pepper
2 cups tomato sauce (see pages 12-13)
2 cups béchamel sauce (see page 12)

1 cup grated mixed cheeses, including Parmesan
pinch of grated nutmeg
¼ cup butter

In southern Italy, fresh ripe tomatoes are always used in cooking for as long as they are available. For the winter months, most households make bottled tomato sauce, made while the sun is hot and tomatoes are cheap and plentiful. If made properly, this can taste exactly like fresh tomatoes picked from the plant.

Cook the *lasagne* four at a time in boiling salted water and lay them carefully on a wet tablecloth to drain so that they cannot stick together. Warm the two sauces separately. Put the grated cheese into the béchamel and melt thoroughly. Season both sauces with salt and pepper, and mix the nutmeg into the béchamel.

Butter an ovenproof dish with one-quarter of the butter and cover the bottom with cooked *lasagne*. Pour over a little of each sauce, and cover with more *lasagne*. Continue in this way until all the pasta has been used up. Be sure to end with béchamel. Dot the rest of the butter over the top of the finished dish.

Bake in a preheated 375° oven for 20 minutes. Rest for 5 minutes before serving.

CANNELLONI RIPIENI DI SOGLIOLA AL CURRI
Cannelloni with Curried Sole Stuffing

A recent invention, this dish is a favorite with English friends who seem to like curry in any shape or form! A very elegant dinner party dish, it is also quite easy to make.

14oz fresh white lasagne
salt
⅓ cup butter
4 medium lemon soles, cleaned and filleted

½ teaspoon medium hot curry powder
4 tablespoons heavy cream
juice of ¼ lemon
2 cups béchamel sauce (see page 12)

Cook the *lasagne* four at a time in plenty of boiling salted water, drain and lay carefully on a wet cloth side by side. Butter an ovenproof dish with a little of the butter. Cook the soles in the remaining butter until the flesh will flake easily. Cool, then flake the flesh and place it in a bowl. Mix the curry powder with the cream and add to the fish with the lemon juice. Mix well. Season with salt and mix one more time. It should be very creamy and thick; if you aren't happy with the consistency, add a little of the béchamel.

Place a couple of teaspoonsful of the fish filling in the center of each sheet of *lasagne*, roll it up and place, joined side down, in the ovenproof dish. Cover each layer of *cannelloni* with béchamel sauce. Sprinkle a very small amount of curry powder over the top.

Bake in a preheated 400° oven for 20 minutes or until well browned and bubbling hot. Serve after resting for 5 minutes.

Right: (top) *Lasagne al Pomodoro al Forno;* (bottom) *Fettucine al Forno*

FETTUCCINE AL FORNO
Baked Fettuccine

Laganelle are the Neapolitan version of *fettucine*, but they are not made with eggs and in Naples can be bought in bakeries. In Neapolitan dialect they are called *lampe e tuone* (thunder and lightning).

A very simple but elegant dish to serve for family or friends. This could not be easier to make, particularly if you buy the pasta ready made from one of the many specialist stores.

14oz fresh fettuccine
salt and pepper
½ cup butter
½ cup grated Parmesan cheese
2 tablespoons hot water

5 tablespoons fine dry breadcrumbs
5oz mozzarella cheese, cubed
4oz best baked ham, sliced into fine strips

Cook the pasta in plenty of boiling salted water, drain while still quite firm and transfer to a bowl. Add half the butter and half the Parmesan and the hot water. Mix together very thoroughly. Butter an oven-proof dish and coat with most of the breadcrumbs. Pour in half the pasta and scatter over the *mozzarella*, ham and a little more Parmesan. Grind over a little fresh black pepper. Cover with the remaining pasta and dot the rest of the butter over the top. Sprinkle on top the rest of the Parmesan and breadcrumbs.

Bake in a preheated 400° oven for about 20 minutes until the top is well browned and crunchy. Serve after resting the dish for 5 minutes.

CANNELLONI CON IL MAIALE
Cannelloni with Pork Filling

1 large onion, peeled and chopped
1 carrot, scraped and chopped
1 stick celery, chopped
1lb lean ground pork
1 tablespoon butter
2 tablespoons Marsala
1oz dried mushrooms, soaked for 20 minutes, rinsed and chopped

3 tablespoons tomato paste
salt and pepper
14oz lasagne (green or white)
1 cup béchamel sauce (see page 12)
3 tablespoons grated Parmesan cheese

As pork takes quite a long time to cook, you should get the filling going before you cook the *lasagne*. Put the onion, carrot, celery, pork and butter into a saucepan and simmer for about 10 minutes, then add the Marsala. Allow the fumes to evaporate, then add the mushrooms and tomato paste. Season with salt and pepper. Simmer for 1 hour. Dilute with a little boiling water if the mixture appears too thick.

Meanwhile, cook the *lasagne* four at a time in plenty of boiling salted water and drain them side by side on wet cloths to prevent sticking.

Fill the *lasagne*, roll them up and lay them in a buttered ovenproof dish. Cover with the béchamel and scatter over the Parmesan. Bake in a preheated 400° oven for 20 minutes or until well browned and bubbling hot. Serve after resting for 5 minutes.

CANNELLONI CON IL MANZO
Cannelloni With Beef Filling

This is a very filling dish, perfect for storing in the freezer and feeding to hungry families and friends. To turn it into a more sophisticated dish, sprinkle slices of ham and button mushrooms all over the top before covering with the béchamel.

14oz fresh lasagne (green or white)
salt and pepper
⅓ cup butter
2oz dried mushrooms, soaked for 20 minutes, rinsed and chopped
1½lb lean ground beef
1 carrot, scraped and chopped
1 large onion, peeled and chopped

1 clove garlic, peeled and chopped (optional)
4 tablespoons Marsala
2 heaped tablespoons tomato paste
1 tablespoon chopped fresh parsley
2 cups béchamel sauce (see page 12)

Cook the *lasagne* four at a time in plenty of boiling salted water, then lay them side by side on wet cloths until you are ready to use them. Put most of the butter, the mushrooms, beef, carrot, onion and garlic (if used) into a saucepan. Fry together very gently until the onion is transparent and the beef well browned. Add the Marsala, raise the heat to evaporate all the alcohol, then add the tomato paste and parsley. Season with salt and pepper. Cook gently until thickened, about 30-40 minutes.

Put a little filling into the center of each sheet of *lasagne* and roll it up. Lay each one sealed edge down in a buttered ovenproof dish, either all in one layer or in several, depending upon the size of the dish. If the filling is very runny, strain it first and save the juices for pouring over the *cannelloni* once they are all arranged in the dish. Warm the béchamel through, pour it over the *cannelloni* and dot the remaining butter over it.

Bake in a preheated 400° oven for about 20 minutes or until hot and bubbling with a golden crust on the top. Rest it for about 5 minutes, then serve with grated Parmesan offered separately.

PARTY PIECES

◆

These recipes are for dishes with which to impress
your friends; they are special dishes, to be prepared
for special occasions. Most require you to be a good
cook, but you can make it all much easier for yourself if you follow the hints which are given. For
example, use frozen pastry; and if you are required
to make a sauce, a filling and the pasta, I suggest you
buy the pasta, make the sauce and filling the day
before and put them together on the day.

All these dishes originated in the days when the
big Italian noble families had about three cooks and
two assistants working in the kitchen; those times
are long gone, but with a little advance planning you
can make the dish look and taste as if your own team
of cooks made it, and also feel as if they did!

VOL-AU-VENT CON TORTELLINI ALLA PANNA
Vol-Au-Vent Filled With Creamed Tortellini

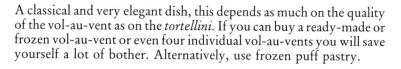

Previous page: Vol-au-Vent con Tortellini alla Panna

A classical and very elegant dish, this depends as much on the quality of the vol-au-vent as on the *tortellini*. If you can buy a ready-made or frozen vol-au-vent or even four individual vol-au-vents you will save yourself a lot of bother. Alternatively, use frozen puff pastry.

FOR THE VOL-AU-VENT
3 cups all-purpose flour
1 ½ cups butter
3 tablespoons cold water
salt
1 egg, separated, to glaze
FOR THE FILLING
3 ½ cups all-purpose flour
4 eggs
salt
4oz ground pork
4oz ground veal
4oz finely chopped cooked ham

1 egg
¼ cup butter
2 tablespoons dry breadcrumbs
⅓ cup grated Parmesan cheese
½ tablespoon chopped fresh
  parsley
pinch of grated nutmeg
salt and pepper
FOR THE SAUCE
⅓ cup butter
1 ¼ cups light cream
⅓ cup grated Parmesan cheese
salt and pepper

Make the vol-au-vent first of all. Make a normal puff pastry with the flour, butter, water and salt. When you have given it its final turn, divide the dough in half. Roll out one-half on a floured board and cut out a round using a dinner plate as a guide. Set this round on a dampened baking tray. Roll out the other piece of dough and cut out another round the same size. Using a smaller plate as a guide, cut a round from the center of this, making a ring and a smaller round. Brush the top edge of the large round on the baking tray with beaten egg and place the ring on top. Press gently to seal. Make shallow incisions, about 1in deep, all around the sides of this vol-au-vent case. Brush the top of the ring, the bottom inside of the case and the top of the smaller round (which will be the lid) with beaten egg. Do not glaze the sides of the case or lid or the pastry will not rise.

Bake in the center of a preheated 430° oven for 20-25 minutes or until golden and well risen. Remove from the oven. Scoop out any soft middle from the case. Leave aside to dry and cool.

Make the pasta dough with the flour, eggs and salt (see page 154). Leave aside in a ball to rest while you make the filling. Fry the pork, veal and ham together in half the butter, then place in a bowl and add the breadcrumbs, cheese, parsley, remaining butter, nutmeg and egg. Season with salt and pepper. Mix with your hands to make a smooth wet paste. Add a little water if too dry. Roll out the dough, fill and seal the *tortellini* (see page 156). Rest for 15 minutes. Cook them in plenty of boiling salted water. Meanwhile, make the sauce. Melt the butter, then add the cream and let it just heat through. Season with salt and pepper and set aside in a warm place.

Place the vol-au-vent in a preheated 425° oven to warm through for 5 minutes. Drain the *tortellini* carefully, transfer to a bowl and pour over the sauce. Mix together thoroughly and allow to cool slightly, stirring at regular intervals to prevent the pasta sticking. If the *tortellini* should absorb too much sauce and become dry, add more cream and melted butter.

Add the cheese and mix once more. Pour into the hot vol-au-vent case. Lay the lid gently on the top and serve.

VINCISGRASSI
Vincisgrassi

The original idea of the dish was to use a whole boned chicken, as each part of the chicken had a different and very particular flavor, and all the different flavors had to mingle and be tasted separately. Sadly, I don't think any part of a modern, mass-produced chicken tastes any different from any other part. So to simplify everything, as it is already quite a complicated dish, we will use three plump chicken breasts. This dish tastes best if made the day before you eat it.

Vincisgrassi is the most typical pasta dish of the Marche region. It is thought that it was invented by the cook of the Austrian General Windisch-Graetz, who held a position of great power in the region during the Napoleonic Wars. The word *vincisgrassi* is an Italianised version of the General's name.

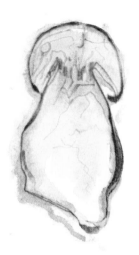

FOR THE PASTA
2½ cups all-purpose flour
¾ cup semolina
2 tablespoons butter
2 tablespoons Marsala
3 eggs
FOR THE FILLING
⅓ cup butter
1 onion, peeled and chopped
2oz dried mushrooms, soaked for
 20 minutes and rinsed
1 black truffle, sliced

4 tablespoons chicken stock
3 plump chicken breasts, boned
 and sliced into strips
10oz chicken livers, chopped
4 tablespoons Madeira
5 tablespoons boiling water
salt and pepper
2 cups very thick béchamel sauce
 (see page 12)
⅓ cup grated Parmesan cheese
1 cup very thin béchamel sauce
 (see page 12)

First make the pasta dough with the flour, semolina, butter, Marsala and eggs (see page 154). Roll it out as finely as possible in one or two sheets and cut it into rectangles, each about 4×6in. Cook the pasta, four or five pieces at a time, in a large pot of boiling salted water, drain and lay them all out separately on a wet cloth until you need them.

To make the filling, melt three-quarters of the butter in a large saucepan (large enough to take the chicken breasts) and add the onion. Fry gently until transparent. Add the mushrooms and allow to stew for a few minutes, then add the truffle. Fry for 5 minutes. Add the stock and leave to simmer for 10 minutes.

Add the chicken breast strips and brown lightly on all sides. Add the chicken livers and fry very quickly until they are no longer red. Add the Madeira, let the alcohol evaporate, then add the boiling water and leave to simmer for 25 minutes.

Season with salt and pepper, and mix in the thick béchamel. Butter an ovenproof dish and cover the bottom with pasta. Pour some of the filling over it and cover with more pasta. Continue in this way until you end up with a last layer of pasta. Sprinkle the cheese between each layer as you go along and dot the remaining butter over the top. Leave the dish to rest for at least 6 hours, preferably overnight.

Cover the top of the dish with the thin béchamel, then bake in a preheated 425° oven for 30 minutes. Serve hot.

ROTOLO DI PASTA FARCITA
Stuffed Pasta Roll

An impressive dish to serve as part of a buffet.

FOR THE FILLING
1lb cooked spinach, chopped
7oz ricotta cheese
⅔ cup chopped best baked ham
⅔ cup grated Parmesan cheese
2 eggs, beaten
pinch of grated nutmeg
salt and pepper

FOR THE PASTA
3½ cups all-purpose flour
4 eggs
salt

TO SERVE
2½ cups tomato sauce (see pages 12-13)
½ cup grated Parmesan cheese

During the Renaissance pasta was often served as an intermediate course between the starters and the meat course. It was usually sweet, having been cooked in a flavored sweet water such as orange blossom or rose water, and dressed with cinnamon, nutmeg, vanilla and powdered sugar.

Mix the chopped spinach with the *ricotta*, ham and Parmesan. Add the eggs and nutmeg, season, mix thoroughly and set aside.

Make the pasta with the flour, eggs and salt and roll it out as normal (see page 154). Finally, roll it out into a large sheet, about 18×12in (depending on the size of your saucepan). Spread the filling over it carefully, to within about 1½in of the edge. Roll it up tightly, then wrap it in a clean white cloth. Tie the ends *very securely*.

Boil a large saucepan of salted water (a fish kettle works very well in this instance) and carefully lower the pasta roll into it – don't let it sag in the center. Boil for 1 hour.

Heat the tomato sauce. Remove the pasta roll from the water, drain it, then unwrap it and slice it neatly on to a platter. Pour over the tomato sauce, sprinkle with Parmesan and serve at once.

RAVIOLI CON CAVIALE ALLA RUSSA
Ravioli with Caviar Russian Style

This very sophisticated dish has a unique flavor.

FOR THE PASTA
3½ cups all-purpose flour
4 eggs
salt

FOR THE FILLING
2lb lettuce hearts
2oz caviar

2 tablespoons heavy cream
salt

FOR THE SAUCE
2 tablespoons butter
1oz caviar
5 tablespoons light cream
3 tablespoons vodka

Make the pasta first with the flour, eggs and salt (see page 154) and set aside to rest.

Cook the lettuce hearts in very little boiling water. Drain and squeeze out all the water, then chop. Mix with the caviar, cream and salt. Fill and seal the *ravioli* as normal with this mixture (see page 156).

Melt the butter, add the caviar and stir gently over a very low heat. Put the cream in another saucepan and warm it gently. Pour the vodka over the caviar and butter and set alight, then add the cream. Mix for a few minutes over a low heat. Set aside in a warm place.

Cook the *ravioli* in plenty of boiling salted water, drain and arrange on a warm platter. Pour over the sauce and serve at once.

Right: *Rotolo di Pasta Farcita*

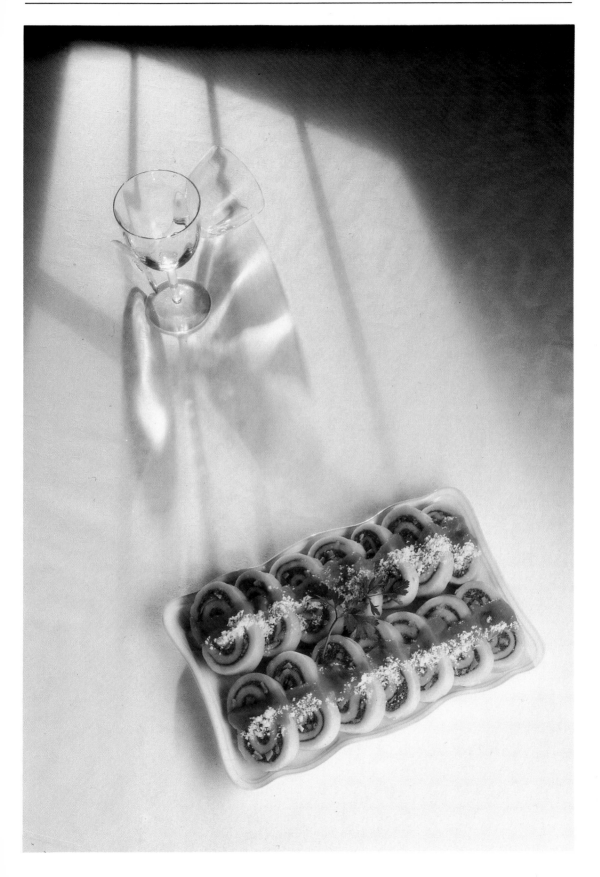

PASTICCIO DI TORTELLINI ALLA BOLOGNESE
Bolognese Tortellini Pie

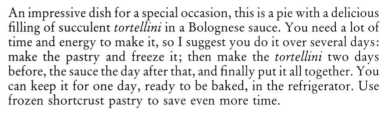

According to Giovanni Poggi, Grand Master of the Fraternity of the Bolognese Tortellino, the *sfoglia* should always be "as light as a caress and as round as the moon".

An impressive dish for a special occasion, this is a pie with a delicious filling of succulent *tortellini* in a Bolognese sauce. You need a lot of time and energy to make it, so I suggest you do it over several days: make the pastry and freeze it; then make the *tortellini* two days before, the sauce the day after that, and finally put it all together. You can keep it for one day, ready to be baked, in the refrigerator. Use frozen shortcrust pastry to save even more time.

FOR THE SAUCE
1 onion, peeled and chopped
2oz prosciutto crudo or unsalted bacon, chopped
1 carrot, scraped and chopped
1 stick celery, chopped
1 clove garlic, peeled and crushed
2 tablespoons oil
8oz ground beef
1oz dried mushrooms, soaked for 20 minutes, rinsed and chopped
4 tablespoons red wine
14oz canned tomatoes, drained and puréed
salt and pepper
pinch of mixed dried herbs
1 tablespoon chopped fresh parsley

FOR THE FILLING
2½ cups all-purpose flour
6 eggs
salt and pepper
4oz ground veal
4oz finely chopped turkey or chicken
1 slice prosciutto crudo (Parma, San Daniele or similar), finely chopped
1 egg yolk
¼ cup grated Parmesan cheese
pinch of grated nutmeg
2 cups béchamel sauce (see page 12)

FOR THE PASTRY
2½ cups all-purpose flour
⅔ cup butter
1 teaspoon salt
6 tablespoons cold water
1 beaten egg, to glaze

Make the sauce first so that you can leave it to simmer (or alternatively make the sauce the previous day). Fry the onion, *prosciutto*, carrot, celery and garlic in the oil until the onion is transparent. Increase the heat and add the beef. Brown it gently, then add the mushrooms. Cook for 10 minutes or until soft. Add the wine and raise the heat to evaporate the alcohol. (When you can no longer notice the odor of the wine it means the alcohol has evaporated.) Add the tomatoes, season with salt and pepper and leave to simmer for at least 1 hour. At the last moment, add the herbs and parsley.

Make the pasta dough with the flour, eggs and salt as normal (see page 156). Combine the veal, turkey or chicken, *prosciutto*, egg yolk, Parmesan and nutmeg, and season with salt and pepper. Mix together to a smooth paste. Use this filling to make the *tortellini* (see page 156). (The alternative is to buy ready-made *tortellini* or *cappelletti* and use them instead.) Leave to rest.

Make shortcrust pastry with the flour, butter, salt and water. Divide into two pieces, one slightly larger than the other. Roll out the large piece and use it to line a buttered deep pie dish (large enough to take all the *tortellini*). Set aside.

Cook the *tortellini* in plenty of boiling salted water, drain and transfer to a bowl. Allow to cool. Pour over half the sauce and half the béchamel and mix together. Make layers of the *tortellini*, sauce and béchamel in the pastry case. Roll out the other piece of shortcrust pastry and lay it on top. Seal the edges very carefully and brush the top with the beaten egg glaze. Pierce the pastry here and there with a needle. Use the pastry trimmings to decorate the top of the pie and glaze these also.

Bake in a preheated 375° oven for 40 minutes or until the pastry is golden brown. You can then either serve it from the pie dish or turn it out on to a platter. Serves 6.

RAVIOLI FRITTI CON ASPARAGI
Fried Ravioli with Asparagus Spears

This dish is a triumph once completed, but it does require quite a lot of hard work, so make sure you leave yourself plenty of time to make it, and that your second course and pudding are very simple and require little or no cooking. Out of season use canned or frozen asparagus.

FOR THE FILLING
1 large eggplant, sliced
salt and pepper
1 onion, peeled and finely
  chopped
⅓ cup butter
½ cup all-purpose flour
½ cup hot milk
4 walnuts, shelled, peeled and
  chopped
2 egg yolks

FOR THE PASTA
3 ½ cups all-purpose flour
4 eggs
salt
oil for deep-frying
TO SERVE
10oz asparagus spears
1 tablespoon all-purpose flour
2 tablespoons butter
2 cups tomato sauce (see pages
  12-13), hot
¼ cup grated Parmesan cheese

Sprinkle the eggplant slices with salt and leave to drain for 2 hours. Rinse and pat dry with paper towels, then cut into cubes.

Fry the onion gently in butter, then add the cubed eggplant and fry until golden. Remove the eggplant and add the flour. Stir until smooth, then add the hot milk, a spoonful at a time. You should end up with a smooth paste so you may need to add more or less milk. Remove from the heat. Add the walnuts and egg yolks, mix together and stir in the eggplant. Mix this filling together very thoroughly, season with salt and pepper and set aside.

Make the pasta dough with the flour, eggs and salt (see page 154) and fill and seal the *ravioli*. Leave to rest for 10 minutes. Deep-fry the *ravioli*, four or five at a time. Drain them on paper towels and pile them high on a warmed platter.

Toss the asparagus spears in the flour, fry quickly in the butter until tender and arrange them upright around the base of the mountain of *ravioli*. Pour the tomato sauce over the top so that it runs down the sides and into the platter. Sprinkle the cheese all over and serve at once.

ALL SHAPES AND SIZES

In order to shed some light on the muddling subject of the many shapes and sizes in which pasta is made, I will attempt to divide it into sections.

Pasta Secca: This is dried durum wheat pasta, which is factory-made with durum wheat flour and water. It is the largest category and comes in an incredible variety of shapes and sizes.

Pasta all'Uovo: The next largest section is that which is made up of *pasta all'uovo*, or egg pasta, which is made from flour and eggs. You can either make this yourself at home, or buy it freshly made in specialist shops and some supermarkets, or you can buy the factory produced variety which is dried and sold ready-packaged. The factory-made egg pasta is quite nice, but it is generally considered that the fresh hand-made article is much better. Egg pasta is also used to make stuffed pasta.

Semolina Pasta: This can also be made from a combination of flour, semolina and water and is dried to a very hard consistency. It can be factory-produced or hand-made and is easily recognizable as it is a different color from other kinds of pasta and has a fine coating of flour on the outside.

Whole Wheat Pasta: This is usually factory-produced except for certain types of home-made whole wheat pasta like *bigoli* or *pizzocheri*.

MATCHING THE PASTA TO THE SAUCE

The subject of which pasta to use with which sauce is a very thorny question as each person you talk to will have their own opinion. There are some classic recipes, such as *Bucatini all'Amatriciana*, the best known sauce to go with that particular type of pasta, but to my mind you should use what is available in the area where you live, what you like and what you have in your pantry. There are no real hard and fast rules, but in the following list I have tried to give guidelines as to which sauces 'sit' best on the various pasta shapes. As you experiment, you will find out for yourself that, as a general rule, rich meaty sauces go best with chunky short pasta; tomato sauces (especially fresh tomato) go best with long thin pasta or small short shapes; olive oil and garlic sauces go best with long thin pasta shapes, including those which are hollow; and sauces which are cream, butter or bechamel based sit very well on small, fine delicate pasta shapes. But as always with pasta, the permutations are endless and ultimately the choice is yours.

The world of pasta becomes very confusing as you try to sort out the names of each shape. For example, nobody can say for sure what a *maccherone* really is. *Maccheroni* is still a generic name for all sorts of pasta shapes, and what is called *maccheroni* in one part of Italy can be called something quite different in another area. Similarly, many of the following pasta shapes have different names in different parts of the country and you will no doubt come across countless other shapes and names. Each manufacturer has a different name for the shapes they produce and, as they invent a new pasta shape each year, it is hard to keep up! But do not worry about it. The important thing is that the pasta tastes good, and here is a short A-Z designed to help you find your way around:

PASTA SECCA

Anellini: a common type of *pastina* (very small pasta). The name means 'little rings'.

Ave Marie: another name for *cannolicchi* or *paternostri*. A small type of tubular pasta which is quite thick and stubby. Used a great deal in soups or in pasta dishes with vegetables.

Bavette: a narrow kind of long flat pasta. They can also be egg pasta. They go well with creamy, egg-based and delicately-flavored sauces.

Bavettine: the same as *bavette* but slightly narrower.

Bombolotti: large concave short pasta, most suitable with ragù and other quite rich sauces containing meat or mushrooms with a tomato sauce.

Bucatini: large thick *spaghetti* with a hole down the center, most traditionally served as *Bucatini all'Amatriciana* or *Bucatini alla Carbonara*. They also go well with all oil and garlic based sauces.

Canelloni: although these are usually home-made with flour and eggs, you can also find a dried flour and water variety available in many supermarkets. They come in the oven-ready type, which you just fill and cook in the oven as usual, or in a type that needs to be lightly boiled first, before filling and cooking.

Cannolicchi: see *ave marie*.

Capelli d'Angelo: very fine *spaghettini*, suitable for children and sometimes put in soups. The name means 'angel's hair'.

Capellini: fine spaghetti, slightly thicker than the above. The name means 'fine hair'.

Conchiglie: means 'shells' and that is what they look like; concave short pasta used with all kinds of sauces, both meat and tomato-based and cheese/cream-based.

Crestoni: also called *creste di gallo*, meaning 'rooster's crest', and that is just what they look like. A very pretty pasta shape that goes well with most meat or vegetable-based sauces, with or without tomato.

Ditali: the name means

'thimbles' and they are the same size and shape as a thimble, except that the end is chopped off. They are shaped like *ave marie* but larger. They go particularly well with fresh tomato sauces.

Ditalini: exactly the same as *ditali*, but half the size. More often used in soups.

Eliche: the name means 'propellors' and that is more or less what they look like. This shape is often wrongly called *fusilli* and goes well with most tomato-based or cheese-based sauces.

Farfalle: 'butterflies': shaped like an open-winged butterfly. These can also be made with egg pasta and go very well with fresh tomato-based sauces.

Fusilli: long hollow *spaghetti* shaped like a spring. They are expensive as the best are hand-made in factories. They go very well with garlic and oil-based sauces, especially those with seafood or tomato. On a restaurant menu you may well see *fusilli* but be presented with *eliche* as they are often confused.

Gnocchi: not to be confused with real *gnocchi*, which are made from potato, pumpkin, semolina or spinach and *ricotta*, this is a concave dried pasta shape rather like a small cupped palm. It is about 1in long and the same across at its widest point. Smooth sauces sit best on this shape, particularly those containing cream or cheese, which cling to the grooved outside and are held succulently in the hollow, scooped-out center.

Gomiti: means 'elbows' and they are rather like a bent variation of *rigatoni*. Use as a change from *maccheroni* or other short stubby pasta.

Gorzettoni: I think these are the largest of all the dried pasta. They are like very big *gomiti*. Best with rich meaty sauces or perhaps stuffed and baked.

Lancette: meaning 'little spears', this is a popular *pastina* (very small pasta) served to children with a very simple sauce or used in soup.

Lingue di passero: these are called 'sparrows' tongues' and are a flat ribbon pasta. Best with delicate, creamy sauces or with fresh tomato.

Linguine: slightly wider than *lingue di passero*, this is another flat ribbon-like pasta which goes well with delicately-flavored sauces. The name means 'little tongues'.

Lumache: these are called 'snails' because they are the same shape as snails' shells. They go well with most tomato and cheese-based sauces.

Maccheroncini: a much smaller version of *maccheroni*, used a great deal in soups and in baked pasta dishes.

Maccheroni: commonly considered to be longish, plump, hollow and tubular, though this same shape is often given many other names. A very popular shape, as they go well with rich meat-based sauces and with equally rich cheese-based sauces.

Maccheroni alla Chitarra: these look like square cut *spaghetti* and are the main speciality of the Abruzzo region. They are very difficult to make at home unless you possess the special *chitarra* that is required to cut them. However, you can achieve almost the same thing if you cut *spaghetti* on a hand-turned pasta machine as they come out square. Otherwise you can buy the factory-produced, dry variety.

Maniche: shaped rather like *ditali*, they are short, wide and tubular and go well with most sauces, though not so well with the oil and garlic-based ones. The name means 'sleeves'.

Messicani: odd shaped pasta, somewhere between *farfalle* and *gemelli*. The name means 'Mexicans' and they are often sold multi-colored (red, green and white). They go well with creamy sauces or simple tomato sauces.

Mezze maniche: half-sized *maniche*.

Molle: small, twisted spring-like shapes which go well with tomato and meat sauces.

Pastina: this is a name for any sort of very small pasta which is given to children or used in soup.

Paternostri: see *ave marie*.

Penne lisce: quite large, short, tubular pasta with the ends cut off diagonally like a quill. The name means 'feathers' or 'quills'. They are very popular with all sorts of sauces, the most famous being *Penne all'arrabbiata*. *Penne lisce* are smooth.

Penne rigate: the same as the above but with a ribbed exterior surface. *Penne* also come in a smaller size, just as wide but a little shorter, which is called *mezze penne*, or half *penne*.

Pennette: a smaller size of *penne*, not to be confused with *mezze penne*. *Pennette* are smaller all round: shorter, thinner and narrower. Very good with delicate sauces and an easy shape to eat standing up at parties.

Pipe: hollow, curved, short pasta with a ribbed surface. Very similar to *gomiti* or *conchiglie*. They go particularly well with cheese-based sauces. The name means 'pipes'.

Pipette: a smaller version of *pipe* meaning 'small pipes'.

Rigatoni: slightly larger than *maccheroni*, they are short, tubular pasta, about 1-1¼in long, with a ribbed surface. They go particularly well with all rich meaty sauces.

Sedanini: small tubular pasta, like small *maccheroni* but ribbed and a little narrower. Perfect with fresh tomato and creamy sauces. The name means 'little celeries'.

Sedani lisce: like *sedanini* but longer and with a smooth surface.

Use the same sauces as you would use with *penne*. The name means 'celeries'.

Sedani rigate: as above with a ribbed surface.

Spaghetti: too well-known to describe.

Spaghettini: finer than *spaghetti*, they go particularly well with fresh tomato and basil sauces.

Stelline: star-shaped *pastina*, very popular with children and in soups.

Tempestina: tiny *pastina* like very small beads. Perfect for very small children, also served in broths as a soup. The name means 'little tempest'.

Torciglioni: twisted, short pasta, quite narrow. As they absorb a

lot of sauce, they go very well with creamy and cheese sauces.

Tortiglioni: the same as *rigatoni*, but slightly bent in the middle. Use with all rich meaty sauces.

Trulli: also called *ruote*, or 'wheels', they are shaped like small cart wheels. Very pretty pasta that go well with pretty sauces! They absorb sauce very well as they are ribbed and of an intricate shape.

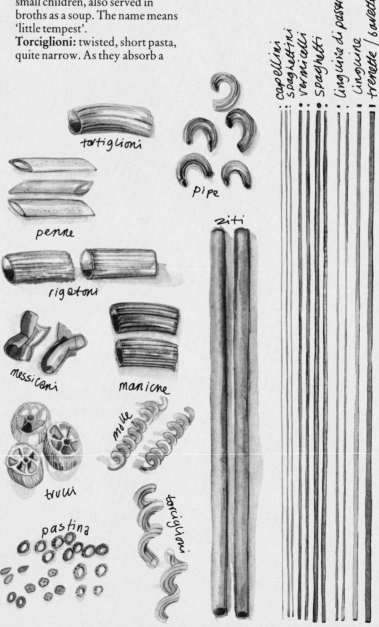

Vermicelli: the name means 'little worms' but they are just a type of long thin pasta, slightly finer than *spaghetti*. Very good with light tomato sauces and seafood.

Vermicellini: half the thickness of the above.

Ziti: these are very long smooth *maccheroni* which you can break off to the required length. Used a lot in baked pasta dishes and in rich meaty dishes. The same type of pasta is sold half as thick and is called *mezza zita*. Not so common nowadays.

Zitoni: double the size of *ziti*.

PASTA ALL'UOVO

The very best egg pasta is that which you make at home, with your own hard work and effort. Experts say that in home-made pasta that is well made you can taste the love a woman has put into it. With a little practice and expertise, you can make fresh egg pasta at home and cut it in any shape that comes into your head. Don't be afraid to invent your own pasta shape and christen it with any name you like.

If you do not have the time or the inclination to make egg pasta yourself, the freshly-made variety now available in shops all over the world is usually very good. The dried factory variety is passable but is really a thing apart. It is the sauce that goes with it which will carry it off more than the pasta itself.

Home-made egg pasta can also be dried and kept for several months with no ill effects, but remember that dried egg pasta will take much longer to cook than the freshly-made variety.

As with any pasta, you can serve egg pasta with any sauce you like, but as it does have a distinctive flavor of its own it is not normal to dress it with strong sauces, heavily flavored with garlic or chili. Meat sauces, however, sit very well on egg pasta, making for a very rich and filling dish. Freshly-made egg pasta should be very pliable and slightly soft; when dried it becomes brittle and must be handled with care.

Egg pasta can be made in a variety of colors. Add a handful of chopped herbs to the egg and flour mixture and you will end up with a nice yellow pasta speckled with green, which is delicious dressed with a creamy white sauce. You can add a little tomato to the mixture for orange/red pasta, beetroot if pink is your color, saffron for an even deeper yellow and spinach for green pasta.

Bassotti: very fine *tagliatelle*.

Bavette: these are thin, flat, ribbon-like and delicate and can be made either of all-purpose flour and water or of flour and eggs. Can be made at home or bought factory-made and dried.

Cannelloni: large flat squares of egg pasta that are rolled up around a filling, covered in sauce and baked. When you buy the ready-made industrial kind they will usually be rolled up with a hollow down the center to fill. When home-made, proceed as if making *lasagne* and then roll them up.

Fazzoletti: a larger variety of *lasagne*. The name means 'handkerchiefs' and they can be made at home or bought ready-dried and prepared for filling.

Fettuccine: thin, ribbon-like strips of pasta, which when sold dried in packages are in bunches rather like birds' nests. About ¼in wide, they can be made easily at home and are available freshly-made in most pasta shops. They go very well with most meaty sauces.

Garganelli: this is a type of hand-made *maccheroni* from the Emilia Romagna region for which you need the original *pettine* in order to get them absolutely right. They should look like oddly-shaped *maccheroni* and should be about 1½in long. The easiest way to reproduce them is by rolling squares of *sfoglia* around a pencil or similar cylindrical shape over an ordinary fine-toothed comb.

Gasse: Ligurian type of pasta which are always home-made.

Gramigna: short, stubby, hand-made pasta used a lot in Reggio Emilia; they look and taste just like broken-up *bucatini*.

Lasagne: large squares or rectangles of egg pasta, often boiled and layered with a sauce or filling and then baked. They can be white or green. *Lasagne* can be bought freshly-made in specialist shops and supermarkets, or dried in packets, or can quite easily be made at home.

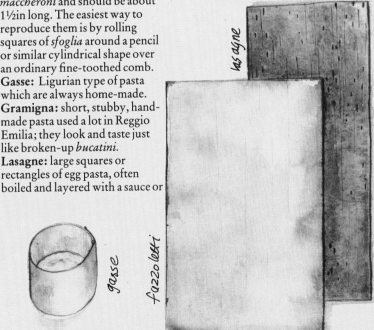

maltagliati

nidi d'angelo

tagliatelle

tagliarini

picagge

Lasagnette: rather wide *fettuccine*, quite often made with curly edges with a pastry wheel. Normally about ¾in wide, they go with many different kinds of sauces. They can easily be made at home and are also available dried.

Maltagliati: these are made in the same way as *tagliatelle* or *fettuccine* except that they are cut on the bias to achieve an uneven triangular shape. The name means 'badly cut' which is what they should look like! Used a lot in soups and baked dishes, they can also be used in place of *tagliatelle* or *fettuccine* for a change.

Nidi d'Angelo/Nidi d'Oro: small clusters of very fine golden pasta, usually used in soups. They are almost impossible to make at home as you would never get them fine enough, so it is best to buy the dried variety in packets. The name means 'angel's nests' or 'golden nests'.

Paglia e Fieno: this is a pretty combination of white and green egg pasta which is cut into ribbons. *Paglia e fieno* can be made with *tagliarini, tagliatelle* or *fettuccine*. The green pasta is made by adding a little spinach to the egg and flour mixture. The name literally means 'hay and straw' and they look and taste good both with smooth creamy sauces and with bright red tomato sauces with or without meat.

Pappardelle: wide ribbons of pasta about 1¼in wide which are cut with a pastry wheel and thus have wavy edges. They can be bought ready-made and dried, or home-made.

Picagge: these are large Ligurian *lasagne* which are layered with sauce but not usually baked. They always have saw edges and are made at home.

Pizzocheri: irregular shapes made with whole wheat and all-purpose flour.

Quadrucci: when you cut out egg pasta at home you will end up with lots of odd-shaped strips and bits and pieces. If you chop these up to small squares and use them to enrich a soup or broth as you might use *pastina*, you have made *quadrucci*.

Tagliarini/Tagliolini: these are very fine *tagliatelle*, about ⅒in wide, which can be made at home, or bought fresh, or factory produced and dried. They are best used in relatively sophisticated dishes using cream and butter or with light tomato sauces.

Tagliatelle: these are well-known, just like *fettuccine* except they are a bit wider. They are best if made at home, though the freshly bought kind are also delicious. Widely available in packages, factory-made and dried to a hard, brittle texture. They go with lots of different sauces, both meat and cream/butter sauces suit perfectly. Not normally cooked with fish, though there are exceptions.

Tajarin: the same thing as *tagliarini* or *tagliolini*. *Tajarin* is the name for them in Piedmont.

Trenette: more or less the same thing as *bavette*, these are about ⅛in wide and are long and flat like ribbons. Used a great deal in Liguria, they are traditionally served with *pesto*. They also suit most of the cream-based sauces particularly well.

pappardelle

lasagnette

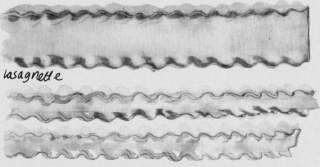

STUFFED PASTA

Stuffed pasta always consists of a shell of egg pasta holding a filling of meat, fish, cheese or vegetables inside it. The finished pockets of pasta with their stuffing are then either boiled or deep-fried, and then dressed with a sauce or just simply with butter and cheese, if required.

Agnolini: similar to *cappelletti*.

Agnolotti: these are a type of stuffed pasta found in Tuscany and in the Marche area and can be made in all sorts of shapes, but most usually like a half moon. They can be bought ready-made with a variety of stuffings.

Anolini: semi-circular stuffed pasta from Parma and the surrounding area. In my recipe I have filled them with a combination of nutmeg and cinnamon, bound with egg and toast. They can, however, be filled with all sorts of different ingredients. It is difficult to find them ready made outside the Parma area so if you want to try them, make them at home.

Cappelletti: small stuffed pasta shapes, usually filled with ham and cheese or minced meat. These are also available in packets in a dried form and are often used in soups. The name means 'little hats' because they look rather like party hats and they are much nicer if freshly made at home. They can also be bought fresh in shops and some supermarkets.

Pansoti: Ligurian *ravioli*. They should be very rounded and plump, but the pasta shell must be triangular.

Ravioli: the most well-known and easiest to make of all the stuffed pastas. They are usually square, with neatly serrated edges. They can be stuffed with all sorts of meats, cheese or vegetables and are also to be found freshly made and on sale in many shops and supermarkets.

Raviolini: the same as *ravioli* but about half the size. The name literally means 'little *ravioli*'. *Ravioli* and *raviolini* can also be green, made with spinach pasta.

Tortellini: these are a slightly larger version of *cappelletti* which are also available in a dried, factory made form. They contain an enormous variety of fillings and can be home-made or bought fresh in most supermarket chains and specialist shops.

Tortelloni/Tortelli: the same as *tortellini* but about double the size.

WHOLE WHEAT PASTA

Bigoli: whole wheat *spaghetti*, typical of the Venice area and often home-made; they are also available dried in most shops or freshly made in some specialist shops. In Mantua, the same name is given to some thick home-made *spaghetti* made with flour and eggs.

SEMOLINA PASTA

Culigiones: a Sardinian kind of *ravioli*, but the pasta shell is made with fine semolina and eggs instead of all-purpose flour and eggs. Most Sardinian pasta is made from semolina flour and water or eggs and in the former case, the pasta has to be very carefully dried before use.

Malloreddus: dry, very hard, small pasta shaped like small sea shells and traditionally Sardinian. They can be made at home, but the package, dried variety is really the best. They are made with water and semolina flour.

Orecchiette: these are made in the same way as *malloreddus* and come from Puglia. You can make them at home if you have the time and patience, but as they have to be dried before use anyway, you may as well buy the ready-made packet variety. They take 20-25

minutes to cook, although a friend of mine tells me that in Sardinia they are often cooked for up to 50 minutes. The name means 'little ears'.

HOW TO MAKE YOUR OWN PASTA

This is a step-by-step guide to making fresh egg pasta at home and by hand: *pasta all'uovo fatta in casa.* If made well, there is nothing quite so delicious, but do not be discouraged if you find it difficult to master the *sfoglia* at first: it is difficult to make, but once you get the knack it becomes simpler and after a few times you will wonder what all the fuss was about.

The fresher the eggs you use, the better the pasta will be. If you try using freshly-laid farm eggs you will really taste the difference. Once made, you can store fresh pasta in the freezer or, in the case of the flat types, dry it carefully on a clean dishcloth, transfer it to a bowl and store it, uncovered, in a cool place; it keeps for up to a month in this way.

One last word of advice before you start: if you are having trouble making the *sfoglia*, cover it with a dishcloth and go away for 20 minutes. Quite often, after a short rest, it will do what you want it to do!

FOR ALL FRESH PASTA

Quantity: For each person, allow 1 egg and ¾ cup all-purpose flour and some salt. These are the basic ingredients, although some people use a little milk or oil to make the dough softer.

1. Pour out the flour on to your pastry board or working surface and shape it into a mountain. Push your fist into the center to make a hollow, then break the eggs into this hollow. Add also the salt, and milk or oil if used.

2. Whisk the eggs together with your fingertips for a minute, amalgamating a little of the flour. Then begin to mix the eggs and flour together using a circular motion. Start from the center and work outwards. Use one hand for mixing and the other hand to hold the mound in place and to prevent the eggs escaping.

3. When all the flour has been absorbed, push and squeeze the mass into a lump of dough. Using both hands, press down with the heel of your palm and begin to pull and knead the dough. Keep turning, kneading and folding until you have a smooth, elastic consistency. When you have achieved this consistency (it should take about 10 minutes) set the ball of dough aside to rest under a dishcloth for 5 minutes. Meanwhile, wash your hands and clean and dry the work surface carefully. Until you are really expert it is a good idea to divide your dough into two or three sections at this point and roll them out separately.

4. Flour your work surface and the rolling pin. Flatten the ball of dough with your hands. Begin to roll it out, always rolling away from you. Turn it slightly after each roll, so that it begins to form a circle. When you have rolled it into as perfect a circle as possible, fold it in half and roll it out again.

Continue in this way until you have achieved a smooth, fine sheet of pasta, about ¼in thick. This is called *la sfoglia.*

5. This is the most difficult part. You must now stretch the *sfoglia* to its maximum capacity. Roll it out as thin as possible, curl the end furthest from you around the rolling pin and roll it towards you, pushing away from you. Work very quickly or the pasta will dry out and become impossible to work with.

6. When you have rolled up about one third of the *sfoglia*, turn it around and roll it away from you. Repeat this process about eight times until the pasta is about ⅛in thick. Flatten any curled up edges with a quick turn of the rolling pin.

At this point, you have a *sfoglia* which is as thin and light as possible. You may now proceed to make flat or stuffed pasta of many different kinds. Some cooks hang the sheet of pasta up to dry at this point, letting it hang over the edge of the table, half rolled on to the rolling pin. I don't think you need to go to these lengths, although it is important to let it dry for a while so that it will not stick. About 20 minutes is usually enough time; as soon as the surface looks leathery it has dried enough. If you are making stuffed pasta you may prefer not to dry it as it will help the edges stick together if it is a little moist.

FOR THIN FLAT PASTA

  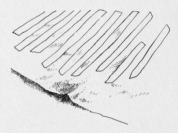

1. Roll up the thin *sfoglia* on itself very gently.

2. Cut to the desired width (see table below) with a steady, sharp knife. It is not unlike slicing a Swiss Roll.

3. Pick up two or three sections of cut pasta by the ends and lay them gently on a clean dishcloth covered with a little flour. Continue in this way until you have cut the whole roll and laid out the strips of pasta. Allow to dry on the dishcloth for about 15 minutes before cooking as usual.

GASSE
Cut the *sfoglia* into strips about 4in long and ½in wide. Take each end of a strip and press together firmly to form large rings. Use a little water to help the ends stick. These rings are *gasse*.

Cutting guide for thin flat pasta	
Lasagnette:	about ¾in.
Tagliatelle:	½in.
Fettuccine:	¼in.
Linguine/ Trenette:	about ⅛in.
Tagliarini/ Tagliolini:	⅒in.
Bassotti:	⅒in.
Capellini:	less than ⅒in.

WIDE FLAT PASTA

PAPPARDELLE

1. Cut the *sfoglia* into long strips about 1in wide, using a pastry wheel to give them their characteristic fluted edges.

2. Allow to dry on clean dishcloths for about 5 minutes, then cook as usual. Remember that *pappardelle* will need twice as much water as usual when you boil them.

LASAGNE

1. Cut the *sfoglia* into neat rectangles about 2¾×3¼in with a sharp knife.

2. Allow to dry on a clean cloth for about 5 minutes, then cook, a few at a time.

PICAGGE

1. Cut the *sfoglia* into rough-shaped *lasagne* with a pastry wheel. They should be approximately 1¾in × 2¼in but the actual dimensions do not matter much as long as they are all roughly the same size.

2. Allow to dry on a clean cloth for 5-10 minutes, then cook them a few at a time.

MALTAGLIATI

1. Roll the prepared *sfoglia* up on itself. Cut across the roll on the bias, first one corner, then the other.

2. Cut straight across the center

to give the pasta roll a straight edge once again.

3. The *maltagliati* open out into a rough shape, each about ½in wide at the widest point. As they

are called *maltagliati* ('badly cut'), this is what they should look like, so it is not at all important if they all are different from one another.

STUFFED PASTA

There are many types of stuffed pasta, but those included here are the most common. Ingredients and quantities for making the pasta are given in the stuffed pasta chapter (see page 109).

The most important thing to remember when making your own fresh stuffed pasta is that the edges must be carefully sealed before you boil them, otherwise you may lose the filling in the cooking.

RAVIOLI

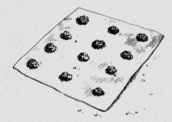  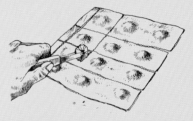

1. Roll out the *sfoglia* to a thickness of ⅛in, then cut it in half. Put a small teaspoonful of stuffing every 1½in or so, in neat rows along one sheet of *sfoglia*. If the pasta seems too dry and you are worried that the shell will not stick, brush the *sfoglia* with a

little water or egg white in between the filling.

2. Cover with the second sheet. Press down very gently with one hand.

3. Roll the pastry wheel along the *sfoglia* in between each mound of

covered filling in both directions, leaving about ¼in around each mound of filling. You should end up with lots of neat squares, each containing a mound of filling. Allow to rest for half an hour. Check they are well sealed at the edges before cooking.

CAPPELLETTI, TORTELLINI AND TORTELLONI

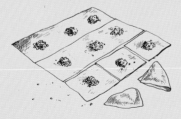 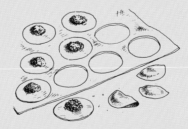 

1. For *cappelletti*, place the filling on the *sfoglia* as if you were making *ravioli*. Set the mounds of filling about 1in apart and cut into neat squares.

2. For *tortellini*, set the mounds of filling 1½in apart, for

tortelloni 2in apart. Cut a circle around each mound. Take each square or circle and fold it into a triangle or semi-circle. Seal the edges with care.

3. Wrap each triangle or semi-circle around your index finger

and press the corners together. A little water might help to stick them.

4. Lay them out side by side on a floured surface and cover with a clean cloth for about 20 minutes before boiling.

AGNOLOTTI

1. Roll out the *sfoglia* as usual. Place the filling on the *sfoglia* in neat mounds about 1¼in apart. Cut a circle around each mound with the rim of a glass or a round cutter.

2. Fold each circle in half and seal the two edges firmly: use a little water if it helps.

3. Press down along the edge to be sealed with the prongs of a

fork to make small indentations.

4. Line them up side by side on a floured surface and cover with a clean cloth. Rest for 30 minutes before boiling as usual.

GARGANELLI

Although traditionally this requires an implement called *il pettine* which is like a large comb, it is possible to make them using a pencil and an ordinary comb, provided the teeth are quite thick and long.

Pasta dough
2¼ cups all-purpose flour
3 eggs
3 tablespoons grated Parmesan cheese

1. Make a hollow in the flour, break in the eggs and also add the

Parmesan. Proceed as usual to make a smooth dough (see page 154). Roll and fold the dough as usual, then finally roll it out to a fine flat sheet about ⅛in thick.

2. Cut out neat squares about 2½ × 2½in, with a sharp knife. Wrap each square around the pencil, pushing down against the comb as you roll to give the *garganelli* their grooves. The easiest way is to lay the comb flat on the worktop, anchor it firmly between two heavy objects and

use both hands to roll and press.

3. Lay the *garganelli* side by side on a floured surface until needed.

ORECCHIETTE

Pasta dough
1⅓ cups semolina
2 cups bread flour
water

1. Mix together the semolina and the flour with enough water to make a stiff dough that is only just pliable.

2. Knead the dough for a long time until really smooth.

3. With your hands, roll the dough into a long thin snake, about ½in thick. Slice crosswise into pieces about ⅛in wide.

4. Take each slice of dough and run it across the table top with your thumb. They should look like small ears or sea shells.

5. Dry carefully on dishcloths for at least 24 hours until hard.

MAKING PASTA WITH A MACHINE

Most Italian housewives possess a hand-turned pasta machine which reduces the time and hard work of making pasta by hand. An inexpensive item, it works extremely well. When using one, you proceed as usual until step three in making the dough, then divide the ball of dough into small sections. Each section is then passed between the rollers on the machine by turning the handle with one hand and feeding the dough through with the other. You repeat this operation five or six times with each section of dough. The result is perfectly smooth and even sheets of *sfoglia* which are then pushed through the desired cutting slot to produce nice, even, well-cut pasta in the most commonly used shapes. The smooth *sfoglia* can also be used to make stuffed pasta.

Another tool available in most Italian kitchens is a Raviolilamp, which looks rather like an ice cube tray. You lay a sheet of *sfoglia* on it, put the filling in each carefully marked square and lay more *sfoglia* on top. Roll the tiny rolling pin over it and the serrated edges automatically cut and seal the ravioli.

ACKNOWLEDGEMENTS

Designed by
Patrick McLeavey & Sue Storey

Photographs by
Charlie Stebbings

Illustrations by
Linda Smith

Food prepared by
Clare Ferguson

Styling by
Liz Allen-Eslore